The Power of Playful Learning:
The Green Edition

By Joyce Hemphill, Laura Scheinholtz,
and Heather Von Bank

Maupin House *by*
capstone
professional

The Power of Playful Learning: The Green Edition
By Joyce Hemphill, Laura Scheinholtz, and Heather Von Bank

Cover Design: Sandra D'Antonio
Book Design: Jodi Pedersen

Library of Congress Cataloging-in-Publication Data
Cataloging-in-publication information is on file with the Library of Congress.

978-1-62521-929-9 (pbk.)
978-1-62521-939-8 (ebook PDF)
978-1-62521-953-4 (ebook)

Maupin House publishes professional resources for K–12 educators.
Contact us for tailored, in-school training or to schedule an author for
a workshop or conference.

Visit www.maupinhouse.com for free lesson plan downloads.

Maupin House Publishing, Inc. by Capstone Professional
1710 Roe Crest Drive
North Mankato, MN 56003

www.maupinhouse.com
888-262-6135
info@maupinhouse.com

Printed in the United States of America in Eau Claire, Wisconsin.
062014 008269

Dedication

This book is dedicated to the families of Dane County and Mankato who attended our play days. Without their support and feedback, none of this would be possible. Also to our spouses, children, family, and teachers who have and continue to support and nurture our playful spirits.

Table of Contents

Foreword
DIY Fun: Making Your Own Fun—Together

Before I get carried away, I need to get a tad theoretical.

There's a book by James Carse called *Finite and Infinite Games*. It's an important book, not only to play scholars and theoreticians, but to people who think play and games have something to do with life.

Fortunately, I'm not going to talk about his book. It's the distinction between finite and infinite that I want to borrow.

The authors of *The Power of Playful Learning* make an admirable effort to describe the educational objectives and uses of each of their games and activities: Admirable because it is sometimes very difficult to tease out all the school-relevant learning that takes place during the making and playing of a game—and even more admirable for the additional activities they've developed that can help parents and children further apply the skills and insights gained during the game to curriculum-related concepts. These efforts offer readers a way to connect all the fun they'll be sharing to educational gains that can easily be shared with the school environment, and further, provide teachers with a way to include the activities as supplements to further reinforce curricular objectives.

These advantages apply to what I invite you to think of as *finite* gains. They are measurable, accountable, relevant to recognized, authenticated, authorized concerns.

But for me—and I hope for all of you who take this book seriously—the far more powerful gains that will be derived from making and playing these toys and games belong to the *infinite* category.

In making something for fun, together, we create moments of immeasurably engaging and enduring connection. We make more than a fun thing. We do more than learn something. We create a shared memory that will keep us together long after the toys and games we make (and some of us) have found their way back to the recycling bin.

And in addition to the educational and economic benefits of making playthings out of scrap and found objects, we learn yet another important lesson: We learn that if we want to have fun, money is truly no object. We can make fun out of anything. All it takes is a little imagination, creativity, ingenuity, love, and time playing together.

As parents, we learn that we don't always have to buy new toys and games to invite our kids to play, that we don't always have to rely on textbooks and homework to invite our kids to learn. As kids, we learn that we don't really need new toys and games. We learn that we have the power to make our own fun, out of anything. We learn that our world is wonder filled and that we can touch, explore, and investigate that wonder in our own family, with the materials at hand.

The idea of playful learning removes the artificial and harmful separation between learning and play, between home and school. The values it conveys and the benefits it offers us are both finite and infinite.

In a way, the phrase *playful learning* is something of a tautology. The very best way we learn is by playing. The very best kind of play leads to a new understanding. And in *The Power of Playful Learning: The Green Edition*, we find invitation after invitation to playful learning at its best.

Bernard DeKoven

Author of *The Well-Played Game,*
A Playful Path, and the Deep Fun website

Introduction

This is NOT a craft book... although it provides instructions for making things using everyday items.

This is NOT a game book... although the things that are made are designed to be played with.

Combining aspects of do-it-yourself with games and activities, this book describes how to make simple games and toys using recyclables and everyday items: "Playing from scratch," as we like to call it. In addition, it includes a listing of the cognitive, educational, physical, social, emotional, and personal benefits a child receives when he or she makes and plays with the toys or games.

The concept for the book was born in 2006 in a different form and since then has been ever evolving. Frustrated with reports of school districts reducing recess time and studies showing parents over scheduling their children in extracurricular activities, three members of the Department of Educational Psychology at the University of Wisconsin-Madison organized a community play event—a **Play Day**—as an effort to educate the community on the benefits of play. By offering activities and space where families could come and play, we were able to highlight the importance of play and promote positive family interactions through play. Thanks to Dane County 4-H, we were given the use of an exhibition hall during the county fair. However, the play event had a budget of zero dollars. With the spirit of the former governor and U.S. Senator Gaylord Nelson, who was instrumental in establishing Earth Day in the United States, we chose to develop and create games using recyclables. After several years of inviting families to play our low- or no-cost activities at the fair, we began to get requests from teachers, childcare providers, and parents for a written collection of what we had done so that they could use them.

Since then, we expanded our efforts and have organized community play events and workshops in Mankato, Minnesota, and Aurora, Illinois. While each play event has its own unique feel to it, such as being held outside with a nature theme, they all share two important elements: 1) they encourage positive family interactions and 2) they use common recyclable or reusable materials. While it may be easy to buy the latest game, we believe there are important merits to creating play from one's natural or familiar environment.

Children benefit cognitively, physically, socially, and emotionally from time spent interacting with peers and adults. And when that interaction involves making things and then playing with them, it is just fun! In the midst of all this fun, children might not even notice that they are learning. Knowledge will be gained by solving problems together and through opportunities for direct teaching, but there will also be underlying opportunities for behavior modeling. For example, children can learn how to take turns and how to avoid being a "sore loser" by observing another's behavior while playing a game. And let's not forget that this entertaining, interactive time can be enlightening for teachers and parents as well. The adults may discover a hidden talent, new knowledge, or certain personality characteristics in children when they play with them.

The creativity involved in constructing playthings and games by using items already in our environment is an excellent vehicle for uncovering these traits. In fact, the children themselves might discover their new abilities as play with recycled items allows us to alleviate fear of failure, a common roadblock to creativity. If a mistake is made, there is likely another cereal box in the recycle bin: Just try again! Creativity can flow even more by thinking about what substitutions can be made depending on the recycled items at hand. In this way, each child could feasibly create his or her own version of an activity, allowing for personal expression and true ownership.

This process all begins by deciding what materials could be used in making toys, games, or activities. The key is to think outside the box… or paper towel tube or plastic milk jug: How else can these objects be used? What else do we see when we look at them? On the flip side, what can we find around the house or classroom that would normally be "trash"? If it is going into the recycle bin, maybe we could use it for something else first. From trash to treasured plaything, both your pocketbook and our environment will thank you.

To these ends, this book should serve as a guide to help teachers, caregivers, and parents build quality playtime with children. The games and activities presented in this book should be seen as a jumping-off point. We have chosen reusable items that we suspect are some of the most popular in households and try to represent play from around the world. However, we do not know what items you have at your disposal; therefore, feel free to substitute materials that are also clean and safe. For example, if one of our games calls for rocks from outside, but you have a surplus of clean aquarium pebbles, use them.

This book is structured so that readers can choose an activity that promotes different types of developmental and educational capacities. For example, in **Chapter 2: Go the Distance**, games and activities focus on skill development related to prediction, measurement, and graphing. In one activity, children and adults can create recycle racers, which are race cars made from paper tubes, and estimate how far the car will travel. Each activity includes specific instructions and lists materials needed to create the item. The majority of the projects are accompanied with a picture or a diagram. In addition, we include a section that describes how children benefit as they create the activity and how they benefit cognitively, emotionally, and/or physically by playing with their creation (play skills). Icons above each game or activity indicate how many people are needed to play, and the **Person-Activity Table** in the back of the book consolidates this listing into one clear visual guide. It includes the number of people needed to play the game or activity and the number of people needed to play the variations. A **Glossary of Materials and Terms** offers further explanations of common materials and definitions of terms, some of which are in bold upon first reference in the book.

We hope this book serves a larger audience than we could ever hope to reach with either our initial Play Day or the ones that followed. So, browse our pages, find your materials, and go play from scratch!

Yours in Play,
Joyce, Laura, and Heather

Note on Safety

Most of the materials listed in this book are household recyclables. Be sure to properly clean the recyclables using warm water and antibacterial soap. In addition to washing, wipe foam egg cartons with a commercial bleach cleansing cloth or with a bleach solution of one tablespoon of bleach per quart of water. Do NOT use egg cartons made from a paper-based material as they cannot be sanitized.

Check all recyclable materials for sharp edges. Those pieces with sharp edges go directly into the recycle bin. Relatedly, some activities require punching holes with a bamboo skewer or sharpened pencil. This should be done with extreme caution. NEVER set an object in your lap or hold it with the other hand when puncturing. Injury can result. Instead, always use a flat surface and place a layer of protection, such as a folded cloth or thick, flat eraser, between that surface and the object being punctured. Encourage children to ask an adult for guidance whenever necessary.

Many of the games and activities contain small pieces, which are a choking hazard to young children, especially those under the age of 3. Please keep these pieces, along with all small objects, out of reach. A toilet paper tube can serve as a choke tube tester. If the item can easily fit into the tube, it is unsafe to give a young child. Also note that an inflated balloon is not a safe item for a young child. Even though it cannot fit into a choke tube tester, a popped or deflated balloon can.

Although we encourage adults and children to work together to design and play with the games, there may be times when adults will need to take the lead especially regarding the use of tools (e.g., craft knife, pliers, scissors). Safety must always be a priority. In addition, some activities are more complex to make than others. Therefore, read through the directions prior to starting the project. Take into careful consideration the ability level of the child and the skill set needed. Then use your best judgment in determining the appropriateness for making and playing the game.

Lastly, when selecting recyclable materials, be mindful that some may cause an allergic reaction. Plastic containers that held peanut butter or nut butter should not be used. Caution should also be used with latex materials, such as balloons.

CHAPTER 1
The Importance of Play

Eight-year-old Miguel is playing outside, stacking boxes that once held kitchen dishes and silverware. Then at once, he knocks them down, only to begin stacking them again.

> **Laura:** *You know, Miguel, at* **play days**, *we have a game called Construction Junction, and it is all boxes. And you can build whatever you want. Do you know how many boxes we get each year?*
>
> **Miguel:** *How many?*
>
> **Laura:** *200!*
>
> **Miguel:** *[eyes wide] Can you smash what you make?*

Every person approaches play differently. Some may look at a pile of boxes and think of building a cabin and playing house while others see it as a chance to test their skills at making the tallest tower ever with the anticipation of watching it tumble and predicting where the boxes might land. Still others, like young Miguel, look at it as a chance to take things apart. What is important is that we all are given the chance to play because of the inherent benefits we get from playful action. From gross motor skill development, to practicing creativity, to improving problem-solving and cooperation skills, children gain valuable experience in play.

This book outlines activity and game suggestions that can help make play a part of one's learning experiences. This first chapter explains some of the characteristics of play, the developmental benefits play provides, and why play should be present in a classroom or learning environment.

Characteristics of Play

For children, play is at the center of development. A baby develops facial muscles and coordination skills for talking and eating by blowing spit bubbles. A toddler gains understanding about causation and movement by rolling a ball down the stairs. A preschooler begins to tackle the challenges of adult roles by engaging in dramatic play. And the school-age child creates problem-solving strategies when playing rule-based games.

Even early psychological theorists acknowledge the important role of play in learning and development. Influenced by the work of Sigmund Freud, Carl Jung (1971) noted that, "The creation of something new is not accomplished by the intellect but by the play instinct acting from inner necessity" (p. 123). Many of Jung's contemporaries echoed his sentiments as well. Lev Vygotsky (1933) suggests that, "Play is the source of development... Action in the imaginative sphere, in an imaginary situation, the creation of voluntary intentions and the formation of real-life plans and volitional motives—all appear in play... ," (p. 16) while, similarly, Jean Piaget (1962) credits play as "... in reality one of the aspects of any activity" (p. 332). Together with noted theorists such as Erik Erikson, Howard Gardner, John Dewey, and Maria Montessori, play has been cited as being responsible for the development of symbolic thought, language, literacy, logical-mathematical thinking, problem solving, imagination and creativity, social-moral development, emotional development, physical development, and the sense of self.

Why do so many experts view play as having a critical role in development? For one thing, play provides an opportunity for children to make sense of their world. Starting with their current understanding, children physically experiment with ideas and combine them with other ideas, which then get integrated into their knowledge base. According to educational reformer John Dewey (1907), "The child's impulse to do finds expression first in play, in movement, gesture, and make-believe, becomes more definite, and seeks outlet in shaping materials into tangible forms and permanent embodiment" (p. 59). Children must act before comprehending the underlying concepts behind an action. The simplest childhood form of acting out ideas is play.

Play is also a time when children *practice skills* they will use throughout their lives. It is not only parents and teachers that argue this point. Professionals in the medical field recognize the pivotal role that play has in the lives of children, particularly in how they negotiate socially through their world, leading to healthier overall development. In his seminal article in *Pediatrics*, Kenneth R. Ginsburg (2007) touts this aspect of play, stating that "Undirected play allows children to learn how to work in groups, to share, to negotiate, to resolve conflicts, and to learn self-advocacy skills" (p. 183). He goes on to cite numerous studies that show "when play is allowed to be child driven, children practice decision-making skills, move at their own pace, discover their own areas of interest, and ultimately engage fully in the passions they wish to pursue" (p. 183). Through self-directed play, children develop healthily; they become the individuals they are meant to be as they practice the skills necessary to be friends, partners, and citizens.

An equally important characteristic of play is that it affords a safe psychological environment in which the child can *take cognitive and emotional risks*. In free and unstructured play, there are few, if any, set rules prior to engaging in the play activity. Children are free to explore without constraints hanging over their heads. In play, the child is not being graded. She is not held to a particular standard. The child is free to be wrong. In an interview following the release of his book, *The Unschooled Mind: How Children Think and How Schools Should Teach*, Howard Gardner argues that children's museums, where people participate in hands-on ways, offer a more authentic learning experience because "... it doesn't matter the first or the second time they do something whether they have any idea as to what the 'right' physical principle is; they're getting familiar with the phenomena in a way that fits their own tempo, learning style, profile of intelligences" (Brandt, 1993). We need to provide learning experiences free from the stigma of failure. Play is an excellent way to do so.

And lastly, play is *intrinsically motivated* and freely chosen. The true benefits of play come from activities that are child driven—that is, the child facilitates the play activity. When we provide this opportunity, we are giving the child a sense of agency, a sense of ownership, and a sense of pride. This helps children create an inner sense of motivation, which is highly coordinated with a larger degree of perseverance. A child truly engaged in free play will be running the show and happy to be doing it. He or she will stick with it, even in the face of potential or actual failure. How often can we say this of other learning situations?

Benefits of Play

Playful learning goes beyond the cognitive development that is often our focus in the classroom. It goes beyond the common conception that it is just a way to blow off steam or take a break. Play enhances and supports some very important areas of child development.

Attention development. What educator doesn't want students who can pay better attention for a longer period of time? Play can help children with attention regulation by requiring them to stay focused on something they enjoy. It can promote concentration, for example, when two children build a box tower together. It can also give children the chance to practice persistence. A child who has the opportunity to build the skill of persistence by trying over and over again to get the box tower to stand may be more willing to practice his or her addition skills. The persistence children develop in play can then transfer to more traditional learning situations in the future (Pan & Yang, 2010).

Language development. All of us can think back to the story we had to write for language arts class—the one with the looming due date and a topic chosen for the class by the teacher. Why was it so daunting when, in our free time, we giggled as we sat with circles of friends, writing a story one sentence at a time, passing the paper from participant to participant? With no set guidelines in the latter example, we were free to explore language on our own terms. It was play that allowed for this; we had agency, ownership, and pride in those stories. For the classroom assignment, we had very little—if any—of those characteristics. When we play, we not only develop literacy, storytelling, and vocabulary skills, but we also develop communication skills, including body language. Teachers can further encourage language development by using playful activities in literacy instruction. These playful activities include making up rhymes and chants and playing popular word games.

Emotional development. Play is an excellent way to enhance emotional skill development. Through play, we can explore attachment: How safe is it to jump to the end of the number line if parents stay at the starting line? We expand emotional knowledge, including mood elevation and regulation: A high-five or "job well done" from teammates in an obstacle course race can often make a world of difference to a child who struggles otherwise in the classroom. We can also practice risk-taking by choosing a more high-stakes strategy during tag and anxiety-reduction skills by falling back on our safe strategy of staying near "base" when the risk creates too much nervousness. Play can be an invaluable way to provide opportunities for autonomy development, such as when each child who creates his or her own movement patterns while dancing to music with scarves learns to take ownership of that creation. Educators, parents, and caregivers can promote emotional play by providing toys that are open ended or do not have a singular purpose, allowing children to make their own play story. Often children will project their own emotions into play: Gracie might be unwilling to admit that she is afraid of the dark, but the puppet she creates could openly and safely carry that trait. Then, Gracie is free to explore her feelings about being afraid of the dark without any negative social consequences. Additionally, playing simple games and activities and providing art materials that encourage children to use their imagination provides the groundwork for creative play environments.

Social development. As play is often thought of as a social activity, the benefits of play on social skills are perhaps the easiest to grasp. Play can encourage cooperation and collaboration, sharing, and turn taking, particularly valuable skills for young children to possess. It can give a child the opportunity to practice empathy, conflict resolution, control of impulses, and leadership skills. Play offers a safe environment for learning to understand boundaries and for exploring social and cultural roles and rules. Lastly, play provides an opportunity to explore the "world of work." Anyone who has ever played house or doctor can attest to this last benefit. Remember that the adults in children's lives often provide the model for the development of social skill and play behaviors, so be mindful of the messages you are sending about gender roles, fairness, and equity, especially in play.

Gross-motor and fine-motor development. Gross-motor, or large-movement, development can readily be seen in play involving sports or whole-body engagement. A child participating in a game of tag, for example, will be practicing eye-foot coordination and movement control. She will be gaining flexibility and balance, muscle strength, and cardiorespiratory endurance. She will also benefit from fat reduction, body temperature regulation, and neurological development. Fine-motor, or small-movement, development (generally with the hands and fingers) is often involved in crafts or tabletop games. When a child creates and plays with the popular paper fortune-teller game, he is utilizing hand-eye coordination, practicing fine manipulation, and gaining skill in dexterity. A child may be proficient in one area of motor development but working to strengthen another. Choosing a particular type of physical game or activity can help children explore these specific areas differently.

Personality, identity, and self-esteem development. For young children, playing can be one of the foremost ways to create and cultivate a sense of self. Play offers the child an opportunity to explore the self as he or she engages in imaginary play with others, discovers boundaries between him- or herself and others through competition, and reinforces individualism through creativity. Children learn sets of skills at which they excel, whether it be mathematics or athletics—or a social skill, like conflict resolution. Play offers the opportunity to develop self-confidence, self-esteem, and self-awareness. It can also lead to a greater understanding of social and cultural roles and norms and is a relatively safe situation in which to experiment with personality traits: "What happens if I speak up more instead of staying quiet?" "Can I get what I want by being nicer?" "I wonder if it's okay to let them know how much I like math."

Of course, we need to remember that, at its core, play is also about having fun and is a child's natural, innate form of learning. If play turns into a chore, an assignment, or a rigidly structured activity, it runs the risk of losing the fun aspect that keeps children engaged. We hope to provide ideas for classroom play that offer the above benefits while remaining enjoyable.

Play in the Classroom (or Play and Learning)

It is a commonly held view that learning is to the classroom as play is to recess. Yet when children are engaged in games and playful activities at recess, they are learning about how to cooperate and take turns. They are learning the rules of games as well as both successful and unsuccessful strategies. They are learning and perfecting skills that enhance physical coordination, strength, and speed. In a very real sense, recess play is an application of what has been learned previously at home and in the classroom. And because of the very nature of play, children are more likely to take positive risks in their learning and applications: "If I ask him to play, we'd have enough for two teams." "What happens if I bounce the ball this way?" "I wonder what kind of games our new classmate used to play in China."

If we can apply what we've learned in the classroom to what we do on the playground, can't we use what we do on the playground for learning in the classroom? The answer is yes. Building off the suggestions of their predecessors, contemporary researchers advocate that playful learning activities complement and support the concepts and skills learned during formal academic time. Cognitive developmentalist Alison Gopnik (2012) passionately talks of children at play as being small scientists, naturally using the scientific method in their play to figure out what's going on around them. Not only do curriculum-related games serve as a tool for memorization and comprehension, they also improve attention span, the ability to understand another's point of view, categorization, abstract thinking, creativity, imagination, interpretation of visual/auditory information, planning, problem solving, reasoning, decision making, and concept mastery. Thus, it is clear why developmental theorists identified playful learning as a key factor in a child's cognitive development: "...the playing child advances forward to new stages of mastery" (Erikson, 1950, p. 222).

In short, the benefits of play promote academic skill development. Games and playful learning activities provide a meaningful, accessible context for the learning of concepts and skills, offer applications for understanding rules and procedures, encourage exploration and discovery, allow children to expand on what they are learning, embolden children to experiment and take risks, afford opportunities for collaborative learning with adults and peers, and allow for the practice of skills. Even in his time, Plato knew that browbeating children into studying was not the best method to engage children in learning; Play was the way.

Conclusion

While a lesson on stacking and smashing boxes might not ever be incorporated into the classroom, we highly recommend that some forms of play make their way into formal learning environments. Remember, not all assignments motivate all students nor will all types of play resonate with each child. Entries in this book include directions and materials lists, along with developmental benefits gained from making and playing with the game or activity. Suggestions for and variations of play are also included as guidelines, but additional supplies required are not included in the materials list. *Play* with the suggestions, and tweak and change in ways that work best for you and your learners.

CHAPTER 2
Go the Distance

Student: *I'm never gonna get fractions. Look at this: I can't reduce 25/100.*

Tutor: *Are you sure? I think you might know more about fractions than you think.*
[Student works a while before arriving at the final answer.]

Student: *Wow, all the way to one-fourth!*

Tutor: *So 25 will go into 100 four times. That makes 25 one-fourth of 100. What's another way of saying one-fourth?*

Student: *A quarter.*

Tutor: *Right. And how many quarters are in a dollar?*

Student: *Four... wait, whoa! That's why they call quarters "quarters"!*

Math is all around us. That is a common response to students when they present the age-old question: "When will I ever use this?" So it makes perfect sense for us to play with math. We might just learn while having fun. Games and activities in this chapter focus on skills related to prediction, measurement, and graphing.

Games in This Chapter:

- **Give Yourself a Hand:** Craft a third hand to help launch a ball to hit a target.

- **Oink, Oink, Cha-Ching! Piggy Banks:** Use recycled materials to make banks—a fun way to talk about finance and saving.

- **Paper Chain Measuring Tape:** Create a personalized standard unit of measurement.

- **Recycle Racer:** Zoom! Fabricate a customized race car that crosses the finish line first.

- **Reuse Choo-Choo:** Construct the classic icon of motivation, industrialization, and Western expansion—the locomotive. (Whistle not included.)

- **Ring Toss:** Try out different types of rings in this toss game.

- **Skateboard:** Make a tabletop skateboard, and race with friends.

- **Snow Snake:** Play an adaptation of a popular North American tribal winter game.

- **Zip Line Balloon:** Design a rocket course and guess how far the balloon rocket will travel.

GIVE YOURSELF A HAND

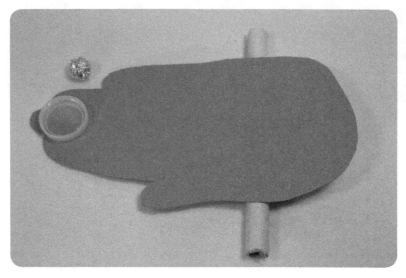

Making Give Yourself a Hand incorporates and utilizes: fine motor skills, focus, hand-eye coordination, self-expression

Playing Give Yourself a Hand utilizes: coordination, gross motor skills, levers, measurement, persistence, potential energy, prediction of angles and distance, problem solving, summation, transfer of energy

Supplies:

- Front or back panel of a cereal box
- Plastic bottle cap
- 5-inch (in) section [12.7-centimeter (cm)] of cardboard tubing from trouser/ slacks hanger
  - ▲ A pencil or bubble tea drinking straw can be substituted
- 4-in x 4-in (10.2-cm x 10.2-cm) piece of aluminum foil
- Plastic deli container (no lid)
- Pencil or marker
- Scissors
- Glue
- Markers for decorating

To Make:

- Trace your hand (with fingers together) on a cereal box.
- Cut out the hand.
- Glue one bottle cap on the fingertips.
- Wad up the foil into a ball.

To Play:

- Place the plastic container on the floor.
- Decide what will be the best place to launch the ball so that it will land in the container. Put the piece of cardboard tubing at that spot on the floor.
- Lay the hand across the cardboard tubing with the fingertip end resting on the surface.
- Place the foil ball in the plastic cap.
- Slap the lower palm to send the ball flying. Did it go in the container? If not, adjust the location of the launcher and/or how the hand has been placed on the tubing.
- To add a personal touch and provide an opportunity for self-expression, decorate the hand.

Note: A double layer of **tagboard** or a craft stick glued to the back of the hand adds sturdiness and results in the ball flying higher and farther.

- -

Suggestions:

- See how high the ball can go.
- See how far the ball can go.
- Try different objects instead of the foil ball (e.g., pom-pom, a bottle cap, a penny, a marble, a cotton ball), and see if they go as far or as high.

Variation:

1. Play a bull's-eye game with friends. Place a piece of paper with a bull's-eye on the floor. Assign points to each ring. Each player is given three foil balls to use. The person with the highest score wins.

OINK, OINK, CHA-CHING!
PIGGY BANKS

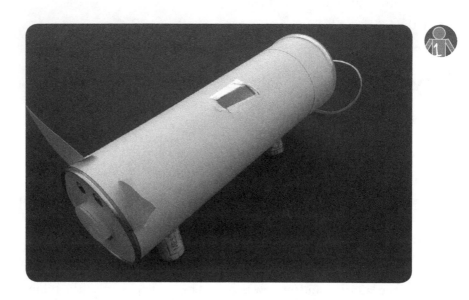

Making Oink, Oink, Cha-Ching! Piggy Banks incorporates and utilizes: creativity, dexterity, imagination

Playing with Oink, Oink, Cha-Ching! Piggy Banks utilizes: arithmetic skill, counting, delay of gratification, dexterity, skills related to thinking about the future

Supplies:

- 1 long tube container with a lid, such as a snack-chip or tennis-ball container
- 2 corks, approximately 0.75 in (1.9 cm) in diameter by 1.75 in (4.4 cm) long or packing peanuts of similar dimensions
- 1 water bottle lid
- 2 sheets of pink construction paper 9 in x 12 in (22.9 cm x 30.5 cm)
- 1 pink (or other color) ribbed ribbon or pipe cleaner, approximately 12 in (30.5 cm)
- Scissors
- Rubber cement
- Markers
- Eraser or folded cloth
- Sharpened pencil
- Tape or glue

To Make:

- Begin with the body of the pig by wrapping the long container with the pink construction paper and securing with tape or glue. When dry, set the container down so that the seam from the paper is on the table. This will be the bottom of the bank.

- Trace a rectangle, approximately 1.5 in (3.8 cm) long and 0.25 in (0.6 cm) wide, on the top of the bank. Very carefully, poke a pair of scissors through the center of this rectangle and cut out the shape. Be aware that too much force can cause ripping if using the chip container. If this happens, tape can be used to mend the rip and more pink paper can cover the piggy's wound. This slot is where the money will go.

- Cut each of the two corks in half so that there are four even pieces. Place these pieces under the bottom of the tube with two at one end and two at the other. These will form the legs. Play with distance from the end to decide what looks best. Glue the legs to the body with the rubber cement. Allow time for the glue to dry.

- Remove the lid from the container. This will be the tail end. Lay the lid flat on the eraser or folded cloth and use a sharp pencil to poke a hole through the middle of the lid. String the pink ribbon, pipe cleaner, or extra paper through this hole so that a little bit of it is on the inside. If using ribbon, tie a knot on the inside so that it won't slip back through the lid. Curl the outside end of the ribbon with a pair of scissors, or use a finger to curl the outside end of the pipe cleaner. Replace the lid with the tail on it.

- Time to make the face. Measure and cut a circle from the pink paper the same diameter of the bottom of the tin and glue it in place. On the inside of the water bottle lid, draw two black dots to make it look like a pig snout. Glue the snout onto the center of the bottom of the container. Use the markers and extra construction paper to create the rest of the features, such as ears, eyes, and a mouth.

- To remove money, remove the lid with the tail in it.

To Use:

- Drop money or folded bills into the slot on the top of Piggy.
- To get money out again, remove the lid with the tail in it.

Suggestions:

- Before using the bank for savings, talk about how much money children think they will be able to save. Making these banks is a fun way to bring real-life practice into a discussion on finances or saving. Have children create a "passbook" (sheet of paper) onto which they enter every deposit in and every withdrawal from their bank. At the very beginning of the book, children should write a prediction for how much they will be able to save each month. Leave space next to that prediction to record how much they really did save.

- Use Piggy to introduce or talk about making graphs. After children have saved for several months, help them create a line graph of how much they wanted to save and how much they did save. Whose lines for saving were higher than their predictions? Whose lines for saving were lower than their predictions? What does that mean?

- Use Piggy to practice counting skills. How many coins have been saved and can now go inside Piggy for safe keeping? Children can count the number of coins as they drop them inside. Or they can count the number of each denomination of coin that goes in—remember that Piggy has an easy-to-open back end so that answers can be double checked or counting can happen again and again.

- To talk about what kind of saving children might want to do, have them create three banks: one for saving, one for spending, and one to give to charity. Decide how much money goes into each. For younger children, this can be done by using one dollar as the whole and saying "10 cents goes to charity, 40 to spending, and 50 to saving." For older children, this is a great way to talk about percentages. If 40 percent goes to spending, how much will they get to spend from a deposit of $7?

- Real money does not have to be used. Fake coins can easily be cut from cardboard. Make sure to mark the coin amount on both sides of the cardboard coin. Fake bills can be made from paper (cardboard will be too difficult to fold and fit into the slot).

Variations:

1. A piggy bank is traditional, but many animals can be represented this way. What sorts of substitutions would be needed to make a horsey bank? How about a lizard bank? What kind of design could be made from a container standing upright?

2. Different types of containers can be used that might suggest a different kind of bank. What about plastic baby formula containers, oatmeal tubs, or well-cleaned condiment squeeze bottles? Where would the money come out and where would the slot be placed to add money to the bank?

PAPER CHAIN MEASURING TAPE

Making the Paper Chain Measuring Tape incorporates and utilizes: calculation skills, dexterity, fine motor skills, following directions, hand eye coordination, patience, problem solving, sustained attention

Playing with the Paper Chain Measuring Tape utilizes: abstract thinking, interpersonal skills when comparing findings, measurement (standard units), understanding fractions

Teachers often use the Rolf Myller book *How Big Is a Foot?* to introduce standard units of measurement. Children then trace their foot on paper, cut it out, and use it to gather linear measurements of various items. What if the child could create a measuring tape? The flexibility of a measuring tape would provide a greater range in obtaining measurements—the circumference of a tree trunk, for example.

Supplies:

- Mailer cards [4 in x 6 in (10.2 cm x 15.2 cm)] that come in magazines
  - ▲ To calculate the number of mailer cards needed, use this information: Each mailer card yields 8 links; there are 27 to 28 links per linear foot.
- Scissors

To Make:

Links

- Cut mailer cards into strips of 0.75 in x 4 in (1.9 cm x 10.2 cm).

- Fold in half the long way to create a 0.4-in x 4-in (1-cm x 10.2-cm) strip and press along the fold with your fingernail to crease.

- Take each end and fold so that they touch at the centerline. Press each fold with a fingernail. Bend the paper so that it looks like a collapsed "V."

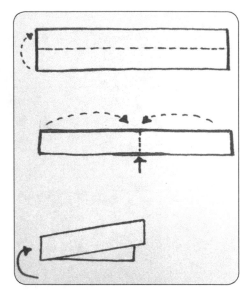

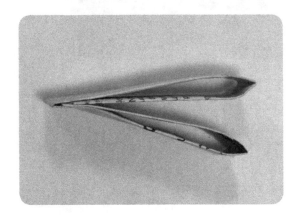

Connect links

- Notice that inside each prong of the "V," there is a slit or loop of paper. Insert each prong into the slits/loops of another link. There is one prong per slit/loop. The addition of each link creates a zigzag design. Add links until achieving the desired length.

To Play:

- Outline your foot on paper. Cut the tracing.

- Make a measuring tape the length of your foot.

- Use both in measuring objects.

- Compare. How are the two tools alike? Different? Are there situations when one is easier to use than the other?

RECYCLE RACER

Making the Recycle Racer incorporates and utilizes: cooperation, creativity, dexterity, hand-eye coordination, measurement

Playing with the Recycle Racer utilizes: different ways of measuring, graphing, prediction, relationships between units of measurement, simple machines (e.g., axles, wheels, ramps), turn taking

Supplies:

- Paper tube, 4–6 in (10.2–15.2 cm) in length and approximately 1.5 in (3.8 cm) in diameter
- 4 soft plastic caps from plastic jugs
- Round bamboo skewer, 12 in x 0.1 in (30.5 cm x 0.3 cm)
- Scissors
- Hole punch
- Large eraser or multi-folded hand towel
- Pliers
- Boxes
- Markers, colored pens, or crayons

To Make:

- Start by creating four holes in the paper tube through which the axles will go. Between 0.5 in (1.3 cm) and 1 in (2.5 cm) from the open ends of the tube, punch the first hole. On the same end of the tube, directly opposite of the first hole, punch another one. Repeat at the other end of the tube. Make sure that the holes line up along the length of the tube.

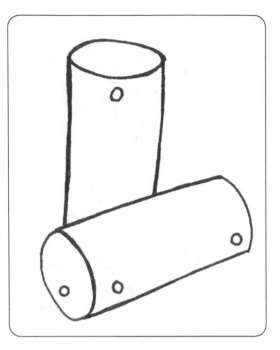

- Place the eraser or multi-folded hand towel on a flat surface. Place the plastic cap on top with the open side down. Identify the <u>exact</u> center of the cap. Place the point of the skewer at the <u>exact</u> center of the cap and firmly press down until the skewer pierces the cap and goes into the eraser or cloth. Do this with all four caps.

- Using the wire-cutting section of the pliers, cut off the sharp ends of the wooden skewer. Then cut the skewer in half.

- Place skewers through the opposing holes in the paper tube. Press a plastic cap onto each end of the skewers to complete the axle-wheel mechanism.*

- Decorate, if desired.

*Axle-wheel options:

These directions use bamboo skewers for the axles, but there are other options. One is to use the plastic stem and platform that are inside frozen push-up treats. For this option, use four of those plastic pieces—since four wheels are needed—and only two axles. Another option is to use drinking straws and soft plastic caps. Make four even cuts into each end of the straw, creating tabs. Flatten out the tabs onto the inside of the cap after inserting the straw, and secure with tape or strong glue.

To Play:

- Cut and/or connect boxes to create a ramp for the racer to roll down.

- Let it roll!

Suggestions:

- Estimate how long each car will roll before stopping.

  ▴ Does the height of the ramp make a difference? Record the results of each run. Graph the results.

  ▴ Does the angle of the ramp make a difference? Record the results of each run. Graph the results.

- Does one racer roll straighter than another? Why might this be?

- Use a longer length of paper tubing. Does length make a difference in motion, distance, or speed?

- Replace the two rear plastic-cap wheels with lids from deli containers. Does this make a difference in distance and/or speed?

- Add weight, such as washers and pennies. Does adding weight make a difference in motion, distance, or speed?

  ▴ Place weight in different areas of the racer. Does the placement of the weight make a difference in motion, distance, or speed?

Variation:

1. Have a race.

   a. Which racer goes the farthest? What might be the reason(s) why one racer goes farther?

   b. Which racer goes the fastest? What might be the reason(s) why one racer goes faster?

REUSE CHOO-CHOO

Making the Reuse Choo-Choo incorporates and utilizes: dexterity, following directions, geometry, hand-eye coordination, measurement, planning, problem solving, spatial relations

Playing with the Reuse Choo-Choo utilizes: gross motor movement, imagination, simple machines (e.g., axles, wheels, ramps), storytelling

Supplies:

- 2 children's shoeboxes with lids (boxes need to be about the same size)
- 2 round bamboo skewers, 12 in x 0.1 in (30.5 cm x 0.3 cm)
- 4 soft plastic caps from plastic jugs
- Paper tube, 4–6 in (10.2–15.2 cm) in length, approximately 1.5 in (3.8 cm) in diameter
- Tissue paper from inside the shoebox
- Scissors
- Hole punch
- Protractor or compass
- Glue or tape
- Marker
- Large eraser or multi-folded hand towel
- Ruler
- Pliers
- Boxes

To Make:

- Remove the lid from shoebox one and set the lid aside.

Adding wheels

- First, create the holes where the axle (bamboo skewer) will slide through. On the long sides of the box, punch four holes toward the bottom corners. The holes should be approximately 0.25–0.4 in (0.6–1 cm) from the bottom edge of the box and approximately 0.5–0.75 in (1.3–1.9 cm) from the end.

  - ▲ Note: If the hole punch doesn't reach that far, undo both end panels by gently pulling open the glued flaps. Cut the inside vertical flaps such that only 0.4–0.5 in (1–1.3 cm) remains. Fold the shortened flaps inside. The hole punch should easily slide over the folded flap now. Punch a hole approximately 0.25–0.4 in (0.6–1 cm) from the bottom edge of the box and approximately 0.5–0.75 in (1.3–1.9 cm) from the end.

- Place the eraser or multi-folded hand towel on a flat surface. Place the plastic cap on top with the open side down. Identify the <u>exact</u> center of the cap. Place the point of the skewer at the <u>exact</u> center of the cap and firmly press down until the skewer pierces the cap and goes into the eraser or cloth.

- Slide this skewer through the box and out the other side. (This skewer will go across the narrow width of the box.)

- Holding the capped skewer in place, attach a soft plastic cap to the other end. (There should now be a secure wheel on both sides of the box.)

- Using the wire-cutting section of the pliers, cut off the end of the skewer, leaving 0.25 in (0.6 cm) extending past the cap.

- Repeat the last four steps for the other axle and wheels.

Engine house support

- The engine house will be box two (lid removed and set aside) inserted perpendicularly into box one. To be sure there is a snug fit, measure the depth of box two. Use that measurement and mark it on the inside of the lid, starting at one of the corners and along the side. Measure and mark the same distance along the opposite length edge of the lid, creating a rectangle. Cut away the rectangle, making sure not to remove the lip of the lid.

- In the remaining section of the lid, locate the middle. Using the compass, draw a circle the diameter of the paper tube. Cut out the circle.

- Place the lid on top of wheeled box one.

Engine house

- Measure and cut away about a third of the length of box two.

Cowcatcher

- Lay the lid from box two on a flat surface. Starting at one corner, using the protractor or compass, draw an arc reaching to the other corner along the width edge of the lid. When cutting out the cowcatcher, include the lid's lip (width end). You'll use this to fasten the catcher onto the train later.

- Draw a thick, black line along the curve of the arc. Starting at the midpoint of the straightedge of the catcher, draw thick lines radiating out to the curved edge.

To assemble

- Insert the cut, short edge of box two into the rectangular opening in the lid from box one. (Box two should now be perpendicular to box one.)

- Insert the paper tube into the circular hole in the lid from box one.

- Attach the cowcatcher using glue or tape.

- Insert the tissue paper into the tube to give the appearance of steam.

To Play:

- Cut and/or connect boxes to create an inclined plane or ramp for the train engine to roll down.

- Let it roll!

Suggestions:

- Estimate how long the train engine will roll before stopping.

  ▲ Does the height of the ramp make a difference? Record the results of each run. Graph the results.

  ▲ Does the angle of the ramp make a difference? Record the results of each run. Graph the results.

- Add boxcars.

  ▲ Take another shoebox and add wheels using the same process as the train engine.

  ▲ Options for connecting the boxcar to the train engine:

    • Tape string from the back of the train engine to the front of the boxcar.

    • Make a small hole in the back of the train engine and the front of the boxcar. Insert a string through the hole and tie a large knot.

    • Insert a metal brad into the back of the train engine and the front of the boxcar. Wrap either a plastic tie or string around both brads.

- How might a boxcar affect the train's motion?

Variation:

1. Have a race.

   a. Which engine goes the farthest? What might be the reason(s) why one engine goes farther?

   b. Which engine goes the fastest? What might be the reason(s) why one engine goes faster?

REUSE CHOO-CHOO

RING TOSS

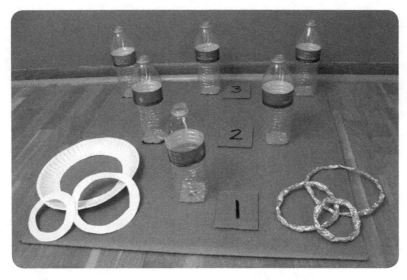

Making Ring Toss incorporates and utilizes: creativity, fine motor skills, measurement, spatial relationships

Playing Ring Toss utilizes: estimation, gross motor skills, hand-eye coordination, healthy competition (group play), prediction, strategy development, summation, turn taking (group play)

Supplies:

- 6 12-ounce (oz) [354.9-milliliter (mL)] plastic bottles
- Duct tape
- Corrugated cardboard box
- Marker
- Scissors
- Aluminum foil
- Paper plates

To Make:

Target

- Take apart the box by cutting off the flaps, and flatten the box to create a large rectangle.

- Tape the plastic bottles (bottle opening up) to the flattened box with the duct tape in the shape of a triangle similar to the placement of bowling pins.

- Using the marker, write out point values on the cardboard to correspond with the placement of the bottles. Higher points should be associated with the targets farthest from the starting line (1, 2, 3; or 5, 10, 15).

Rings—Experiment with different types of material to make rings.

- Twist sheets of aluminum foil into rings. Make sure they fit easily around the bottles.

- Cut out a round center from a paper plate to create a ring.

To Play:

- Designate a starting line with a piece of tape on the floor.

- Toss the rings made of different materials at the targets and try to get the rings on each bottle. Are some rings easier to toss and aim successfully at the targets?

Suggestions:

- Guess how far the rings will fly by moving the starting line closer to or farther from the targets.
- What other materials could be used to create rings?
- Experiment with different shapes of rings. For example, form the shape of a square using aluminum foil or cut a square out of the center of a paper plate and trim the plate edges to create a square ring.
  - Does the shape affect the accuracy achieved? Why or why not?
  - Does the shape affect the distance? Why or why not?

Variations:

1. Play in teams, similar to **darts**, where the teams have to add up scores to reach a point value (e.g., 100) (Masters Games., 2012).

2. In teams, players start at 100 and have to subtract points using the values associated with the original ring toss game. Be the first to reach zero.

RING TOSS

SKATEBOARD

Making the Skateboard incorporates and utilizes: creativity, dexterity, hand-eye coordination, measurement, self-expression

Playing with the Skateboard utilizes: cooperation, healthy competition skills, measurement, prediction, simple machines (e.g., axles, wheels, ramps), social interaction

Supplies:

- Tagboard or cardboard
- Scissors
- Drinking straw
- Round bamboo skewer, 12 in x 0.1 in (30.5 cm x 0.3 cm)
- 4 soft plastic caps from plastic jugs
- Large eraser or multi-folded hand towel
- Tape or glue
- Pliers
- Decorating tools, such as crayons, markers, stickers, glitter, etc.
- Boxes

To Make:

- On the tagboard, draw the shape of a skateboard (elongated oval) that is 6 in (15.2 cm) long and 2 in (5.1 cm) wide. Cut out the skateboard, decorate it, and set it aside.

- Cut a drinking straw into two 2-in (5.1-cm) pieces. Tape these pieces under the front and back of the skateboard, 1.5 in (3.8 cm) from each end; they are the axles. Set aside.

- Place the eraser or folded towel on a flat surface. Place the plastic cap on top with the open side down. Identify the <u>exact</u> center of the cap. Place the point of the skewer at this point and firmly press down until the skewer pierces the cap and goes into the eraser or cloth. Run the skewer through each cap so that the hole becomes just big enough to fit around the widest part of the skewer. Repeat with the other skewer.

- Using the wire-cutting section of the pliers, cut or snap off the pointed end of the skewer and discard. Cut or snap the remaining skewer piece in half. Place skewers through the straws on the skateboard. Press a plastic cap onto each end of the skewers with the edges facing out to complete the axle-wheel mechanism.

To Play:

- Cut and/or connect boxes to create a ramp for the skateboard to roll down.
- Let it roll!

Suggestions:

- Estimate how long each skateboard will roll before stopping.
  - ▲ Does the height of the ramp make a difference? Record the results of each run.
  - ▲ Does the angle of the ramp make a difference? Record the results of each run.

- Have a skateboard race. Which board goes farthest and/or fastest? What might make one board go farther or faster than another?

- Does one board roll straighter than another? Why might this be?

- Try changing the shape of the skateboard. Does this affect the speed, distance traveled, or trajectory of the board?

- How might a rider be added to the board? Will this affect the board's motion?

Variation:

1. Have a race.
   a. Which board goes the farthest? Why might one skateboard go farther?
   b. Which board goes the fastest? What might one skateboard go faster?

SKATEBOARD

SNOW SNAKE

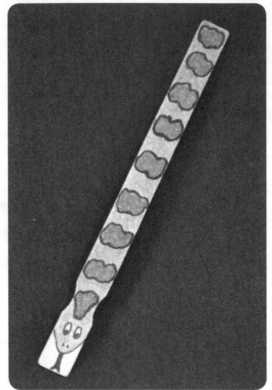

Making the Snow Snake incorporates and utilizes: creativity, cultural exploration, decision making, dexterity, hand-eye coordination, science education (e.g., types of snakes, role of camouflage)

Playing with the Snow Snake utilizes: concentration, coordination, different ways of measuring, graphing, healthy competition skills, laws of physics (e.g., relationship between force and motion), locomotor skills, prediction, relationships between units of measurement, strategy development, turn taking

Snow Snake is a North American tribal game traditionally played outdoors during the winter. The snake is a flat, narrow, and smooth piece of wood that is 3–9 feet (ft) (91.4–274.3 cm) in length. One end often has the head of a snake or bird carved into it (Toth, 2008). The snake is thrown low to the ground so it can readily slide on ice or a smoothed track made in the snow. The person whose snake goes the farthest is the winner.

Supplies:

- Wooden paint paddle
- Permanent markers

To Make:

- Research tribal designs or types of snakes.
- Decorate the wooden paint paddle with markers.

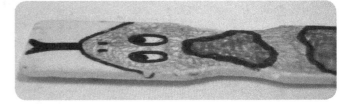

To Play:

- This version of the game can be played indoors or outdoors as long as the surface is smooth.

  ▲ If played indoors, the snake is released underhand, low and toward a wall. The winner is the one whose snake is closest to the wall without touching the wall.

  ▲ If played outdoors, the winner is the one whose snake goes the farthest.

Variations:

1. If space allows, time the glide of the snake. The winner is the one whose snake glides the longest.

2. Use two types of measurement simultaneously, such as distance and time. Is the snake that glides the farthest also the snake that glides the longest amount of time?

3. If space is limited, gently toss a ball or beanbag. Where it stops is the target. The individual whose snake is closest to the target gets to toss it next.

SNOW SNAKE

ZIP LINE BALLOON

Making the Zip Line Balloon incorporates and utilizes: concentration, fine motor skills, hand-eye coordination, manipulation, planning

Playing with the Zip Line Balloon utilizes: decision making, discovery, goal setting, healthy competition skills, hypothesis creation and testing, measurement, Newton's Law of Motion, problem solving, strategy development

Supplies:

- String (cotton string—no polyester) or fishing line
- 1 or more balloons
- Drinking straw (with the bendy part removed)
- Painter's tape
- Clothespin or binder clip

To Make:

Prepare the balloon

- Take two pieces of painter's tape approximately 12 in (30.5 cm) long, and stick them to the underside of the straw (which the string will later be threaded through). Be sure that the pieces of tape are long enough to tape to the balloon when inflated.

The course

- Find a location where a long piece of string can be strung between two posts (or even trees if the game is set up outside).

- First, tie one end of the string to the first post.

- Thread the string through the straw, making sure the straw moves easily along the string.

- Then tie the other end of the string to the second post. The angle of the rocket course can be varied to go up, down, or across.

To Play:

- Blow up a balloon and clip the end of the balloon closed with either a clothespin or binder clip to keep the air inside.

- Bring the balloon over to the first string rocket post, and then stick it to the straw by adhering the tape around it.

- Release the clothespin or clip and watch the rocket go.
  - ▲ Measure how far the balloon went.
  - ▲ Time how fast it took the balloon to reach the end.
  - ▲ Compare the results with others.

- -

Suggestions:

- Try using balloons of different shapes (long cylinder vs. oval) or sizes.
  - ▲ Does shape affect distance? Does shape affect speed?
  - ▲ Does size affect distance? Does size affect speed?
  - ▲ Compare your results with others.

Variation:

1. Set up two courses and race a friend.

CHAPTER 3
Forethought

Mai (10 years old): *Kanshee (7 years old) and I got stuck in my room at Dad's house yesterday.*

Laura: *What? How did that happen?*

Mai: *I was curious about how the doorknob worked, so I took it off from the inside of the room, and the other side fell off the outside of the door.*

Laura: *Oh my! How long were you in there?*

Mai: *Dad left us in there for 15 minutes to teach us to think about these things better next time. But we had two emergency exits figured out!*

Kanshee: *Yeah, I'm small, so I could fit through the vent thingy.*

Mai: *And also there's a window.*

Laura: *Pretty smart problem-solving girls. Did you learn anything new about doorknobs?*

Mai: *Not really, no. Only about escaping.*

Games and activities in this chapter focus on skills related to planning and the development and use of strategies. Whether these problem-solving skills are to escape from the room we've locked ourselves into or to figure out the most efficient way to plant a garden or to find the correct solution to a math problem, the more children practice, the easier it will be to reach the goal. Granted, all games and activities involve thinking, or cognition at some level, but the games in this section push children to focus on details. As children participate in sorting tasks, use mnemonic strategies, or create and test solutions to problems, they will be so engaged and active in the game that they may not realize they are learning!

Games in This Chapter:

- **Achi:** Compete in a strategy game believed to have been created in Ghana. It is similar to the game tic-tac-toe but with a twist.

- **Ball in a Cup:** Think about weight and motion while trying to perfect a method for getting the ball in the cup every time.

- **Bowling:** Explore elements of motion, friction, and resistance by playing a full-sized or tabletop version of bowling.

- **Bring 'em Home:** Design and create a handheld maze.

- **Discus Bull's-Eye:** Make discs to toss at a target.

- **Kick the Wicket:** Arrange the playing field and develop tactics to play this 19th century game.

- **Knucklebones:** Apply grouping skills and fine motor ability to challenge yourself with a game played around the world.

- **Mancala:** Practice counting with a game considered to be one of the oldest in the world.

- **Mini Golf:** Use household items to create miniature golf courses anywhere.

- **My Mini Market:** Re-create the grocery shopping experience on a scale more friendly to children.

- **Peanut Plunge:** Play a unique game of skill that won't be forgotten.

- **Puzzles:** Create a one-of-a-kind puzzle.

- **Senses of Touch:** Make and play a game that uses all the senses.

ACHI

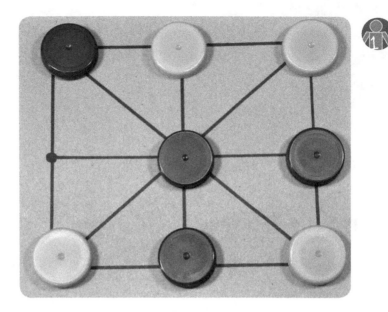

Making the Achi game board incorporates and utilizes: following directions, hand-eye coordination, measuring

Playing Achi utilizes: conflict resolution (in the event of a disagreement), decision making, following rules, planning, prediction, strategy development, turn taking

Achi is believed to have been created in Ghana. It is a simple strategy game for two players whereby the object of the game is to get three game pieces in a row (Sierra & Kaminski, 1995).

Supplies:

- Front or back panel of a cereal box (make sure there is no printing on the back of it)
- 8 plastic caps from bottles or jugs
  - ▲ 4 caps of one color, 4 caps of a different color
- Ruler or straightedge
- Marker

To Make:

- On the back side of the box panel, draw a 9-in x 9-in (22.9-cm x 22.9-cm) square using a ruler.

- Mark a dot at every 3 in (7.6 cm) on each line.

- Connect all the dots so that the board resembles the picture.

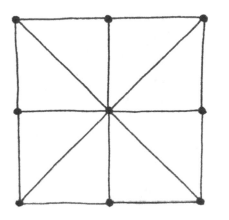

To Play:

- Players take alternating turns placing each of their four pieces anywhere on the game board at points where two or more lines intersect.

  ▲ If a player gets three pieces in a row, he or she is the winner and the game is over.

  ▲ If neither player has three pieces in a row, the game continues. Players take turns moving their pieces along the lines to the next available point of intersecting lines. The game ends when one person gets three in a row.

- Note: Pieces may not jump over another as in the game checkers.

ACHI

BALL IN A CUP

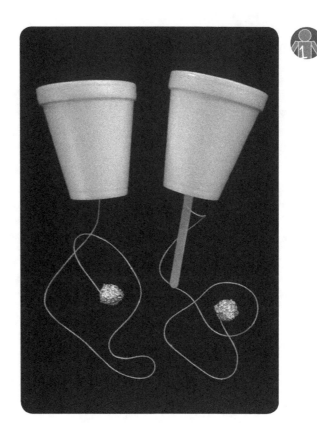

Making Ball in a Cup incorporates and utilizes: dexterity, hand-eye coordination, measurement

Playing Ball in a Cup utilizes: hand-eye coordination, healthy competition skills, math skills (counting, percentages, etc.), persistence, strategy development

Supplies:

- Disposable drinking cup
- 18-in (45.7-cm) length of string or yarn
- Sharpened pencil
- Aluminum foil
- Tape

To Make:

- Begin by turning the cup upside down on a flat surface. While holding the cup firmly on the flat surface, very carefully and slowly poke the tip of the pencil through the center of the bottom of the cup. Do not push the pencil all the way through. The hole should be just big enough to fit the string through. Remove the pencil.

- Holding the cup in one hand, thread the string partway through the bottom of the cup into the inside of the cup. Tie a knot in the part of the string that came through the inside, leaving 1–2 in (2.5–5.1 cm) of string after the knot. When the knot is tied, pull the string so that the knot rests on the inside of the bottom of the cup. Tape the remaining 1–2 in (2.5–5.1 cm) of string to the inside of the cup to help prevent the knotted string from slipping.

- Crumple some foil to make a small, 1-in (2.5-cm) ball. Tie the loose end of the string tightly around this ball. Wrap more foil around the attached ball so that it is 1.5–2 in (3.8-5.1 cm) in diameter. The final ball can be rolled on a flat surface to make it smoother.

To Play:

- Hold the cup in one hand, letting the ball on the string dangle below.
- Using only the hand holding the cup, flip the ball up into the cup.
- Find the best strategy for getting the ball into the cup every time.

Suggestions:

- Count how many times the ball lands in the cup and how many times it misses. What percentage of the time does the ball make it into the cup?

- Is the game harder or easier with a smaller cup?

- Is the game harder or easier with a bigger cup?

- What different materials could be used to create the ball? Does the type of material make the game harder or easier?

Variation:

1. The traditional game uses a cup on a stick. For this version, instead of poking a hole in the bottom of the cup, use scissors to carefully cut a small slit—slightly smaller than the width of a craft stick. Tape the end of the string to the end of the craft stick. Slide the end of the craft stick with the string attached through the slit in the bottom of the cup from outside to inside. There should be about 0.75–1 in (1.9–2.5 cm) of the craft stick inside the cup. Make sure that the rest of the string still hangs outside of the cup. The stick might need to be reinforced by taping to the inside or outside bottom of the cup, depending on how snugly it fits. Proceed according to the above instructions for making the ball. To play, hold by the stick.

BALL IN A CUP

BOWLING

Making the Bowling set incorporates and utilizes: dexterity (filling the bottles), hand-eye coordination

Playing Bowling utilizes: coordination, gross motor skills, healthy competition skills, problem solving, social interaction, spatial relations, strategy development, summation, turn taking

Supplies:

- 10 16-oz (473.2-mL) plastic water bottles
- Sand, small pebbles, grass, crumpled junk mail, water, etc. (enough to fill the bottles)
- Newspaper
- Roll of painter's or masking tape

To Make:

Bowling ball

- Make a sphere that is 3 inches (7.6 cm) in diameter by wadding up newspaper and wrapping it with painter's or masking tape. Take extra care to make sure the surface is nice and round, without a lot of bumps.

Bowling pins

- In an area that can get dirty—outside, for example—put materials, such as sand, small pebbles, grass, junk mail, water, etc. into the water bottles. Each bottle should only contain one type of material, but the bottles do not have to be completely full. One way to easily get sand or dirt into a bottle is to make a temporary funnel out of a piece of paper. Roll the paper lengthwise into a tube and then begin to roll it tighter at one end. It will naturally form a funnel. Insert the small end into the top of the bottle and let it unfurl. Slowly add the sand or dirt into the top of the funnel.

To Play:

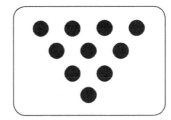

- Now choose a space to set up the alley and, at one end of the lane, place the 10 pins in a triangle as follows:

- Follow the regular rules of bowling.

Suggestions:

- Use balls of different sizes and weights (e.g., bouncy rubber balls, soccer balls, or golf balls).

- Make and use a ball out of an old T-shirt or socks.

- Place number values on each pin, from 1 to 10. Players must then add the numbers on pins they knock down to get their score.

- Using the number values on each pin, each player starts with a score of 55 and subtracts the number he or she knocks down. In this case, the lowest score wins.

- Other numbers may be used following the above directions. For example, using pins numbered 5, 10, 15, 20, 25, 30, 35, 40, 45, and 50 and playing such that lowest score wins, each player would start with a total of 275 and subtract the values on the pins he or she knocks down.

Variation:

1. Play a tabletop version in which a smaller tape ball is used. Pins are made out of cleaned travel-size toiletry bottles (shampoo, conditioner, lotion, soap, etc.). Fillers can be made from the materials listed above, though substitute rocks with small pebbles, such as clean aquarium gravel. The entire game can be contained in a shoebox. Simply remove the lid of the box and cut a door into one of the short sides: Starting from the top open end, make two even cuts down to the bottom. Do not cut this door out on the bottom; rather, leave it attached and bend it down toward the outside of the box. This will be the starting point when playing. When the game is over, the door can be folded back up and held in place by the shoebox lid, keeping the pins and ball inside.

BRING 'EM HOME

Making the Bring 'em Home board incorporates and utilizes: creativity, decision making, dexterity, fine motor skills, planning, spatial relations

Playing Bring 'em Home utilizes: attention regulation, concentration, hand-eye coordination, problem solving, physics (e.g., relation between incline, movement, and the direction of objects), strategy development

Supplies:

- Individual serving-sized yogurt, fruit, or pudding cup
- Shoebox lid or cardboard box lid
- Pieces of tagboard, such as ends from boxes
- Masking tape or duct tape
- Scissors
- 1 to 3 marbles (small balls can be made instead from 2-in x 2-in (5.1-cm x 5.1-cm) squares of aluminum foil)

To Make:

- Using scissors, cut an archway [0.75 in (1.9 cm) wide and 1 in (2.5 cm) high] somewhere along the open rim of the yogurt cup. Turn the container upside down, place it anywhere on the inside of the box lid, and tape it down making sure NOT to apply tape in front of the archway.

- Bend and adhere tagboard to create obstacles for the marbles to go around.

To Play:

- Put the marble inside the box lid and maneuver it until the marble goes through the opening of the cup.

- Start with one marble at a time. As skill improves, put two marbles in the box lid and then all three.

Suggestions:

- Cut more than one archway in the yogurt cup. The more archways, the more challenging the game.

- Put two yogurt cups in the box. Play with two marbles, and maneuver a marble into each cup

BRING 'EM HOME

DISCUS BULL'S-EYE

Making Discus Bull's-Eye incorporates and utilizes: cooperation, coordination, gross motor skills, measurement

Playing Discus Bull's-Eye utilizes: coordination, gross motor skills, healthy competition skills, problem solving, social interaction, strategy development, summation, turn taking

Supplies:

- 8-in (20.3-cm) paper plates or pie tins, two per player
- Roll of colored painter's tape
- Markers or pens
- Flat cardboard, old file folders, or plastic packaging pieces that will stand upright, one for each square created

To Make:

Bull's-eye

- Locate the center of the playing surface and tape a square around it measuring 2 ft x 2 ft (61 cm x 61 cm). In the center of the square, write "100" with tape or use the pieces of cardboard, file folders, or plastic pieces to form a three-dimensional score placard. Write the score on the placard and tape it to the ground. Cardboard and folders can be folded roughly 2 in (5.1 cm) at one end to form a base to tape to the ground.

- Tape a second square outside of this square measuring 8 ft x 8 ft [2.4 meters (m) x 2.4 meters (m)]. Inside this square, write "50" with tape or use a placard.

- Tape a third square outside of the second square measuring 12 ft x 12 ft (3.7 m x 3.7 m). Inside this square, write "10" with tape or use a placard. Feel free to keep going as large as the playing field will allow, always decreasing the point score for the bigger square.

Discus

- Each player takes two paper plates or pie tins and faces them toward one another to create a hollow area inside. If plates are thin, stack two to three plates on each side to make both faces of the discus stronger.

- Tape the plates together.

- Each player writes his or her name on both sides of the plates. This is the discus.

To Play:

- Players take turns throwing their discus. Points earned are equal to the number labeled in the square in which the discus lands. Each player should keep track of his or her own points.

- Play continues to a predetermined score. The first player to reach that score is the winner. Players must decide in advance what this score is for each round. They may also decide to institute special rules. For example, if one player tosses his or her discus into the 50-point range and the next player does the same, do the points for the second player double? This would make the 50-point target, *for that turn*, worth 100 points for the second player.

KICK THE WICKET

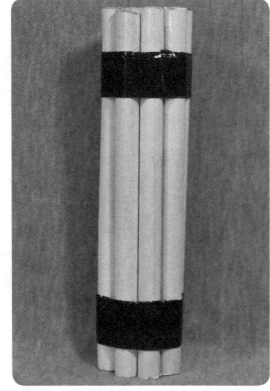

Making Kick the Wicket incorporates and utilizes: collaboration, decision making, fine motor skills, measurement, planning, social skills

Playing Kick the Wicket utilizes: cooperation, coordination, gross motor skills, healthy competition skills, strategy, turn taking

Kick the **Wicket** is a street game that was popular in large cities along the East Coast of the United States beginning in the mid-1800s (Calia, 1891). The game is a modification of a street game that children played in Europe prior to immigrating to North America. While each major East Coast city had its own unique version, the essence of the game remained the same (Calia, 1891).

Supplies:

- 5 cardboard tubes from dry-cleaner trouser hangers, 15.5 in x 0.4 in (39.4 cm x 1 cm), cut in half
- Duct tape
- 3 to 5 plastic containers (one for each base), such as deli containers or yogurt cups

To Make:

Wicket

- Make a wicket by bundling all 10 cardboard tubes together.
- Secure the bundle with duct tape 1 in (2.5 cm) from the ends.

Playing field

- Because Kick the Wicket is a street game that is readily modified depending on location and number of players, a big component of the game is in the planning and decision making prior to the start of the game.

- Select an open area that accommodates running and safe play.

- Select the location for home base and two, three, or four bases, and mark these spots with a plastic container.

  ▲ The number of bases and the distance between the bases depend on the available space and number of players. Note: Kick the Wicket is a street game so there are no set field dimensions. As a guideline, use the dimensions for youth kickball: 40 ft (12.2 m) for 4–5-year-olds, 50 ft (15.2 m) for 6–8-year-olds, and 60 ft (18.3 m) for 9–14-year-olds (Schleyer, 2013).

- Think about and establish rules.

  ▲ If there are base runners and the kicker is called out, can the base runners continue on to the next base or must they return to their starting point?

  ▲ Should runners be allowed to advance to more than one base at a time, or are they limited to one base at a time?

  ▲ If the kicker misses the wicket on the kick, may he or she try again?

  ▲ What if "It" catches the wicket before it hits the ground? Does the kicker automatically become "It"?

  ▲ How do you know when the game is over? Is it when everyone has had a chance to score a point? Is it when someone reaches a certain number of points? How many points?

To Play:

- One person volunteers to be "It," or the catcher, and the other players are the kickers. The kickers decide who will kick first, second, and so on.

- Stand the wicket on its end at home base. The first player kicks the wicket and runs to the first base. The "It" runs to retrieve the wicket, returns it to home base, and shouts out the runner's name.

  - ▲ If a player is successful getting to base before "It" shouts out his or her name, the next player is up to kick. When the next player kicks the wicket, the person on base advances to the next base.

  - ▲ If a player does not reach the base before "It" shouts out his or her name, "It" becomes a kicker and the runner becomes "It."

- A player earns a point when he or she has run all the bases and returns home.

Suggestions:

- Does the wicket go farther if it is kicked at the bottom, middle, or top?

- Does the wicket go higher if it is kicked at the bottom, middle, or top?

- Which increases the kicker's chance to get to the first base: A wicket kicked far or a wicket kicked high?

- Where on the field is the best location for "It" to stand? What other strategies does the catcher need to consider?

- If there is ample space, have two "Its," or catchers. How does this change the kicker's strategy?

KNUCKLEBONES

Making Knucklebones incorporates and utilizes: comparing and contrasting, counting, decision making, measurement

Playing Knucklebones utilizes: attention regulation, grouping, hand-eye coordination, planning

In the United States, Knucklebones is primarily known as "Jacks," but variations of the game are played around the world. Depending on the region, the original game used rocks or the knucklebones of pigs, goats, or sheep (Good, 2012).

Supplies:

- 6 to 11 small, marble-sized pebbles

To Play:

- Decide on the number of pebbles to play with. (A beginner should start with 6 and increase the number of stones as ability improves.) Select one of the stones as the "catcher." The "catcher" will be gently tossed vertically in the air.

- The player sits on the floor and gently drops or scatters the remaining stones on the floor in front of him or her.

- The "catcher" is gently tossed up in the air. While it is in the air, the player picks up one pebble and then, using the same hand, catches the "catcher." If the "catcher" is successfully caught, the picked-up pebble is placed in a "keeper" pile next to the player. Repeat tossing the "catcher" in the air, picking up a pebble, and catching the "catcher" with the same hand.

  ▲ If the player is not successful, all the pebbles, including the "catcher," are gathered and the game starts over.

- Once all the pebbles have been picked up one at a time, the player gathers the "keeper" pile, gently scatters the pebbles on the ground, and begins again. This time, the pebbles are picked up in groups of two while the "catcher" is in the air.

- This pattern continues with the player picking up groups of three pebbles for round three, four pebbles for round four, and so on. By the end of the game, a skilled player would be able to successfully pick up all the stones while the "catcher" is in the air and finish up with catching the "catcher" (Grunfeld, 1975).

Suggestions:

- Pick up pebbles in increasing amounts with each successive toss. Thus, pick up one pebble with the first toss, two pebbles with the second toss, three pebbles with the third toss, and so on.

- Pick up pebbles in sets of odd or even amounts but without a predetermined number. Try to get all the pebbles picked up with the least amount of tosses.

- Use a variety of objects as the "catcher." Try a small ball, a piece of fabric, a bottle cap, a pencil eraser, and a wad of aluminum foil.

  ▴ Which "catchers" make the game easier to play? More difficult?

  ▴ Why do certain "catchers" make the game easier or more difficult? Is weight a factor? Is shape a factor?

MANCALA

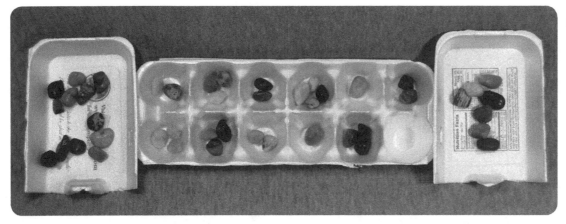

Making the Mancala board incorporates and utilizes: fine motor skills, hand-eye coordination

Playing Mancala utilizes: concentration, face-to-face social interaction, hand-eye coordination, healthy competition skills, planning, problem solving, strategy development, turn taking, visual tracking

It is believed that Mancala is one of the oldest games in the world. The word "mancala" means "to transfer" in Arabic, which describes perfectly how the game is played (AbleMedia, 2000).

Supplies:

- Foam egg carton
- 48 marbles, pebbles, or buttons (color is not important)
- Scissors

To Make:

- Thoroughly wash the egg carton with warm water and antibacterial soap or bleach water and let dry.

- Cut the top off the egg carton.

- Cut the top in half to create the two "stores" for the game. The bottom half is the game board and the split top half is where the pieces are stored.

- Cut off the tabs that keep the carton lid closed and discard.

To Play:

- Object of game: The player with the most game pieces (marbles, pebbles, or buttons) in their "store" wins.

- Players face one another, with the Mancala board between them, and place four game pieces in each of the 12 holes.

- Each player has a "store" (half of the egg carton top) at the end of the Mancala board directly in front of them.

- The game starts with a player picking up all the pieces in any one of the six cups on his or her side. Moving counterclockwise around the entire Mancala board, the player deposits one piece in each of the holes, sequentially, until all pieces in that play have been deposited. Then it's the next player's turn.

  - ▲ When a player crosses over his or her own store, he or she deposits one piece in it.

  - ▲ When a player crosses over his or her opponent's store, he or she skips it.

  - ▲ If the last piece a player drops is in his or her own store, he or she gets a free turn.

  - ▲ If the last piece a player drops is in an empty hole on his or her side, he or she captures that piece and any pieces in the hole directly opposite.

  - ▲ Players place all captured pieces in their store.

- The game ends when all six spaces on one side of the Mancala board are empty. The player who still has pieces on their side of the board when the game ends takes those pieces.

- Players count all the pieces in each store. The winner has the most pieces.

MINI GOLF

Making Mini Golf incorporates and utilizes: coordination, creativity, estimation, gross motor skills, measurement, planning, spatial relations

Playing Mini Golf utilizes: angles, attention regulation, control, coordination, gross motor skills, patience, prediction, problem solving, spatial relations, strategy development, summation

Supplies:

- Long paper tube (e.g., wrapping paper tube)
- Sponge
  - ▲ Note: Use a clean sponge for this activity. When finished playing, reuse the sponge for washing dishes.
- Balls of various sizes OR crumpled newspaper or scrap paper
- Plastic cups or canisters of various sizes and shapes
- Plastic container lids
- Paper tubes (e.g., wrapping paper rolls, cardboard tubes from trouser hangers)
- Cardboard boxes and tissue boxes
- Foam egg cartons
- Books or other flat surfaces (e.g., pieces of cardboard)
- Water hose(s)

>*Supplies continued*

- Individual serving-sized yogurt, fruit, or pudding cups
- Round bamboo skewers, 12 in x 0.1 in (30.5 cm x 0.3 cm)—enough to use as little flagpoles for each hole
- Paper
- Pencil
- Scissors
- Duct tape
- Stapler

To Make:

- This activity works best outside but could be set up in a gymnasium or room with lots of floor space.

- Using duct tape, attach the sponge to the long paper tube to serve as the golf club.

- On paper, design and plan the shape of the golf course. Think about fun challenges along the course and indicate where they will go. Examples of challenges include:

  ▲ Putting the ball through an egg carton tunnel

  ▲ Maneuvering the ball around obstacles, such as cups set upside down in a random pattern or groupings of paper tubes

  ▲ Hitting the ball through a zigzag section made from paper tubes

  ▲ Tapping the ball up and down a ramp made from pieces of cardboard and a stack of books

- If indoors, use the various boxes, foam egg cartons, and/or paper tubes to create a barrier or bumper for the golf course. If outdoors, use the water hose(s) to form the desired shape.

  ▲ Set up the golf course obstacles.

- Use the plastic containers, paper cups, and/or canisters as holes, being sure to tape them to the ground as well.

- Identify each hole with a flag:

  ▲ Make a flag by taping a triangular piece of paper onto the unpointed end of a bamboo skewer.

  ▲ If outdoors, insert the pointed end of the skewer into the ground next to the hole.

  ▲ If indoors, create a flag holder by inserting the pointed end of the skewer through the exterior center point of the yogurt cup's bottom. Set the flag and holder next to the hole.

To Play:

- Estimate or guess how many strokes each hole will take.

- Count the number of strokes that it takes to get the ball in the hole.

- Subtract the estimated number from the actual total.

Suggestions:

- Guess how the ball will change course depending on the angle at which the ball hits the obstacles.

- Experiment with different-sized balls. Does the size of the ball affect the game? If so, in what way(s)?

- Figure out a way to set up the mini golf course to ensure a hole-in-one.

MINI GOLF

MY MINI MARKET

Making My Mini Market incorporates and utilizes: categorization, collaboration, cooperation, decision making, estimation, fine motor skills, gross motor skills, literacy, measurement, planning

Playing My Mini Market utilizes: arithmetic skills, communication skills, cooperation, decision making, economics (e.g., currency, **exchange**), imagination, gross motor skills, literacy, planning, problem solving, role-playing, social interaction

Supplies:

- A collection of large shipping boxes of different lengths and heights, and not taller than the children in all dimensions
- Reusable cloth, paper, or plastic grocery bags
- Used boxes from pasta, rice, crackers, cookies, etc.
- Used containers from condiments, yogurt, sour cream, ice cream, etc.
- Used cans, with lids SAFELY removed, from vegetables and fruit
- Construction paper
- Tissue paper in various colors
- Large, flat cardboard or tagboard
- Markers
- Scissors
- Tape—both masking and transparent adhesive
- Play money*

To Make:

- The large shipping boxes will be the displays for grocery items. If there are particularly large boxes, items can be placed on top of them, as one sees in produce or bakery sections of the grocery store. Smaller boxes can be stacked to create a shelf effect. Before stacking, remove the flaps from one end of the box, and stack boxes on top of one another on their side with the open ends facing out. Boxes can be taped together to make shelves more stable or left unsecured to create a more modular environment. Items can now be placed on these shelves.

- Using leftover cardboard or other tagboard, draw, color, and cut out fruits, vegetables, meats, and cheeses. Note: Packaging from these real items is not safe to use in the mock grocery store. Also take this time to create sale signs and signs for various areas of the store (e.g., Produce, Bakery, Deli, Butcher, etc.).

- Make sure that all reusable boxes, containers, and cans are well sealed and well-marked. If labels have been removed from tin cans, construction paper can be used to wrap the can and label its contents. It will be easier to draw on the paper before attaching it to the can with tape. Tissue paper can be used to fill old condiment bottles: red for ketchup, yellow for mustard, green for relish, white for mayonnaise, etc.

- Now arrange and stock the shelves. Important factors include: how to arrange each section (e.g., how much space needs to be between displays), what items go in each section and why (does bread go with rice and pasta or somewhere else?), and which sections should be near or far from one another for shopping ease. Don't forget a box near the front of the market to hold the reusable bags for shoppers to fill.

- Lastly, price the items. Using masking tape and a marker, write the price of each item and stick it to the item. Pay attention to how each item is priced. A big box of pasta shouldn't cost more than a small box. If prices change, new tape can be placed over the old tape.

----

*Fake bills can be made from paper, and fake coins can easily be cut from cardboard. Make sure to mark the amounts on both sides of the bills/coins.

To Play:

- At a basic level, this store should operate like a real grocery store.

- Players can take in shopping lists and find what they need or just browse. They may also role-play jobs, such as cashier, produce stocker, or deli manager.

Suggestions:

- What other sections could be included in the store: greeting cards display (how would the rack be created?), floral shop, or even a modern addition—a coffeehouse? Before creating the mock store, have children go to a real grocery store and write down all the sections it includes.

- Will the store have coupons or other discounts?

- Give students a budget and have them create a menu for dinner. They must buy all the items needed for the dinner but stay within the budget.

- One large box, or an extra desk or table, can be the checkout counter. Cashiers can use paper and pencil or calculators to find the total price and to figure out how much change is due.

PEANUT PLUNGE

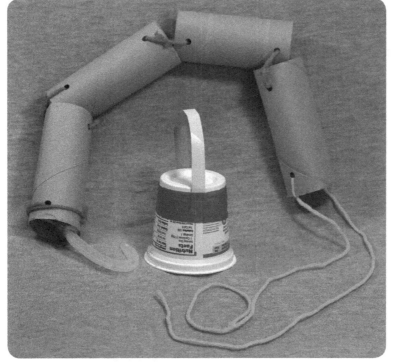

Making Peanut Plunge incorporates and utilizes: dexterity, fine motor skills, measurement, patience, planning, sustained attention

Playing Peanut Plunge utilizes: attention regulation, collaboration, communication skills, concentration, flexibility, gross motor skills, hand-eye coordination, healthy competition skills, movement control, patience, persistence, problem solving, strategy development

Supplies:

- 3 paper towel tubes cut into thirds
- Hook portion ONLY from a molded plastic hanger used at retail stores
- String or yarn
- Individual serving-sized yogurt, fruit, or pudding cup
- Strip of cereal box or other tagboard, 5 in x 0.5 in (12.7 cm x 1.3 cm)
- Scissors
- Hole punch
- Duct tape

To play this game, make a peanut and an elephant trunk.

To Make:

Peanut

- Place the yogurt cup upside down on table. Tape one end of the strip of cereal box close to the cup's bottom.

- Tape the other end of the strip directly across from it, creating a loop. The loop needs to be big enough for the hook on the end of the trunk to readily snag it.

Elephant trunk

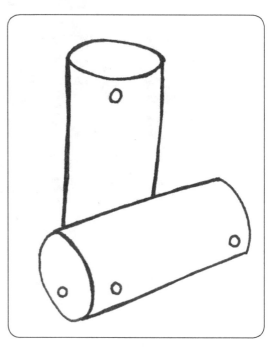

- On one end of the paper tube, punch a hole 0.5 in (1.3 cm) in from the end of both sides. At the same location on the other end, do the same. Continue in this manner for all of the paper tube sections.

- Prepare the hook.

  - Check the hook from the plastic coat hanger for sharp edges. Remove any sharp edges.

  - Take a 1-ft (30.5-cm) length of string, lay it on the table, and place the cut end of the hook in the middle of the string. Tie a knot around this end.

  - Secure the string using duct tape.

- Attach the hook to one of the sections of paper tubing.

  - Take one end of the string that the hook is on and lace it through one of the holes in one section of paper tube. Tie a knot.

  - Take the other end of string, lace it through the opposite hole of that section of paper tube, and tie a knot.

  - Snip any long strands.

  - Note: When held by up by the tube, the hook should hang down from the midpoint of the tube's opening.

- Attach segments.

▲ Next, connect the tube with the hook to another section using a 2- to 3-in (5.1- to 7.6-cm) piece of string. Thread one end of the string through a hole in one section and the other end of the string through a hole in the other section. Tie. Repeat on the other side of the tube.

▲ Continue connecting tubes until there are three or four tubes tied together in a strand with a hook dangling at one end.

▲ At the opposite end of this strand is a tube opening with holes punched on the end. Take a 1.5-ft (45.7-cm) length of string, thread one end through one of the punched holes, and tie a knot. Take another 1.5-ft (45.7-cm) piece of string and do the same with the other hole.

To Play:

- Two players are needed for this game. Each player must have a trunk and a peanut.

- Identify the starting point (home) and the location where the peanut is to be dropped off (reservoir).

- Place the peanut at the starting point.

- Each player ties the trunk around his or her face so that the opening of the tube is over his or her nose.

- Using ONLY the trunk, pick up the peanut, carry it across the room, and set it down. Note: This is a hands-free game. Hands may not guide the trunk.

- Return to the starting point. The first person to transport the peanut to the reservoir and return home is the winner.

Suggestions:

- Make trunks of different lengths. Is the challenge easier with a longer or shorter trunk? Why?

- Make and play with three peanuts. The winner is the first person to transport all three peanuts to the reservoir.

Variations:

1. Form teams and have relay races.

2. To practice communication skills, partner with another person. Person 1 is the carrier and wears a blindfold and his or her own trunk. The partner is the guide. The guide stays next to the carrier and provides directions and information on picking up the peanut and transporting it to the reservoir. Once the peanut is deposited in the reservoir, the carrier removes the blindfold. On the return, the roles switch. The guide becomes the carrier and dons a blindfold and his or her own trunk to carry the peanut safely back home.

PUZZLES

Making Puzzles incorporates and utilizes: creativity, fine motor skills, hand-eye coordination, imagination, spatial relations

Playing with Puzzles utilizes: decision making, dexterity, hand-eye coordination, part-whole relationships, problem solving, spatial relations, strategy development, understanding of shapes

Supplies:

- Cereal box or other tagboard packaging with colorful images and pictures
- Scissors
- Paint, markers, or crayons (optional)

To Make:

- Cut out the front or back portion of the cereal box or other tagboard packaging.

- Cut around the images and lettering to create the puzzle pieces.

Suggestions:

- For an easy puzzle, make fewer pieces. For a challenge, create a puzzle with many pieces.

- Using the plain reverse side of the cereal box portion, create an original design. Then cut the picture into puzzle pieces.

Variation:

1. Switch and put together friends' puzzles.

PUZZLES

SENSES OF TOUCH

Making Senses of Touch incorporates and utilizes:
creativity, decision making, fine motor skills

Playing Senses of Touch utilizes: collaboration, deduction, integration of senses, speculation, tactile knowledge, verbal skills, vocabulary

Supplies:

- Small paper bags (at least a few per participant)
- Scissors
- Items from around the house—for example:
  - ▲ Button
  - ▲ Cut-up kitchen sponge
  - ▲ Key
  - ▲ Piece of cloth
  - ▲ Pillow stuffing
  - ▲ String or floss
  - ▲ Water bottle cap
  - ▲ Wooden block

To Make:

- Line up the paper bags on a table or on the floor.

- Fill the bottom of each bag with a different item.

- Take another bag and cut out a square-shaped opening in the bottom. Make sure the square is big enough to fit a hand through.

- Cover each paper bag containing an item with a bag with the opening. This allows participants to reach into the bag repeatedly without seeing inside.

To Play:

- Each player makes his or her own bags filled with household items.

- Players guess the items in their opponent's bags.

- The objective of the game is for players to use as many different adjectives as possible to describe the item.

- After the player makes a guess, he or she can take the item out of the bag to determine if he or she was correct.

CHAPTER 4
Amalgamation Incorporated

"Not sure what you're doing this morning, but Bella and I are busy hiding out under the covers from the Hulk Raganizer. He likes to eat red hairs and blonde hairs. Wish us luck fighting the monster that lives in our mudroom. Oh, and by the way, he's made from wood and cardboard, tastes like gum, and swabs the deck every day."

—Bella's mom

If little girls are made of sugar and spice and everything nice, then we suppose it's reasonable to assume monsters are made from wood and cardboard. Knowing what parts combine to make a whole is an important aspect of developing creativity. The more we understand how different things fit together, the more options we will have to create something new. Bella and her mother have created a deck-swabbing, mudroom-dwelling, spearmint monster in their imagination. We have included activities that guide children to create things like musical instruments, puppets, and shape games. The entries in this chapter incorporate imagination and creativity with skills related to putting things together and how wholes are comprised of parts.

Games in This Chapter:

- **Cereal Box Weaving Loom:** Construct a simple weaving loom, and then design and make woven pieces using symmetry and measurement.

- **Creative Castaways:** Pretend you are on a deserted island and create tools for survival using recycled materials.

- **Graphic Notation and Musical Instruments:** Create original music compositions and perform using handmade instruments.

  - ▲ **Balloon Bass Guitar**

  - ▲ **Box Harp**

  - ▲ **Buzzy Harmonica**

  - ▲ **Drums**

  - ▲ **Kazoo**

  - ▲ **Rockin' Cereal Box Guitar**

  - ▲ **Shakers**

  - ▲ **Straw Pan Flute**

  - ▲ **Tweeter**

- **Look and Find:** Make this game to play with friends.

- **Puppet:** Express creativity when making a paper sack puppet.

- **Story Cards:** Generate ideas for creative storytelling.

- **Tangrams:** Craft a set of tangrams to explore shapes and geometry.

CEREAL BOX WEAVING LOOM

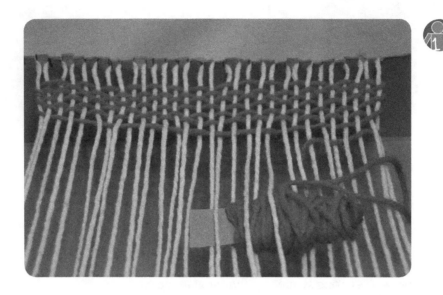

Making the Cereal Box Weaving Loom incorporates and utilizes: fine motor skills, hand-eye coordination, measurement, planning, symmetry

Playing with the Cereal Box Weaving Loom utilizes: counting, creativity, decision making, dexterity, fine motor skills, hand-eye coordination, patience, pattern recognition, sense of self, sequencing

Supplies:

- Cereal box
- String
- Yarn and/or ribbons of different colors and types
- Ruler
- Scissors
- Tape

To Make:

- Using the cereal box's original three-dimensional shape, glue or tape both ends.

- Remove the front of box.

- In the opening of the long panels, measure and mark 2 in (5.1 cm) from each corner. From these 2-in (5.1-cm) markings, measure and mark every 0.25 in (0.6 cm).

- Cut 0.25-in (0.6-cm) slits at each mark.

- Create the **warp** or strings on the loom:

  ▲ Tie a knot at one end of the string and tape it to the back of the box.

  ▲ Insert the string into the first slit and extend it to the slit directly opposite.

  ▲ Wrap the string behind the box and insert into the second slit. Extend the string across the opening to the slit directly opposite.

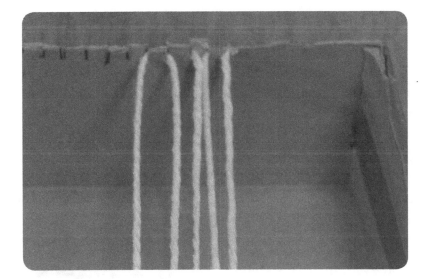

- Continue this process until all the slits have been filled.

  ▲ Be mindful not to pull the string too tight across the box, which will cause the sides to pull in.

- After the last slit, tape the end of the string to the back of the box.

To Play:

Weave

- Using colorful yarn as the **weft,** thread it over and under alternating strings of the warp. (The weft is perpendicular to the warp.)

- When one end is reached, pass the yarn under or over the last crosspiece and begin a new row, continuing the over and under pattern but opposite the previous row. After finishing a row, use fingers to push the weft up next to the previous row. In the event that the weaving material runs out or if a change in material is desired halfway through, new yarn can be tied onto the original piece and weaving can continue.

- Finish the edges of the woven piece.
  - ▲ Turn the box loom over, and cut each strand of the warp.
  - ▲ Starting on one end, gather the strands of the warp in groupings of two to four. As a grouping, tie a knot. Repeat with all the groupings.
  - ▲ Trim.

Suggestions:

- Use smaller looms, wider tabs, and fewer notches with younger weavers.

- Apply tape to the end of the yarn for easier handling while weaving.

- Make and use a **shuttle** for significantly long lengths of yarn.
  - ▲ To create a shuttle, cut a 1-in x 4-in (2.5-cm x 10.2-cm) rectangle from the leftover tagboard.
  - ▲ In one end, make a 1-inch (2.5-cm) cut.
  - ▲ Insert one end of the yarn through the slit, and wrap the yarn around the shuttle.
  - ▲ As the shuttle moves over/under each strand of the warp, unravel the yarn from the shuttle.

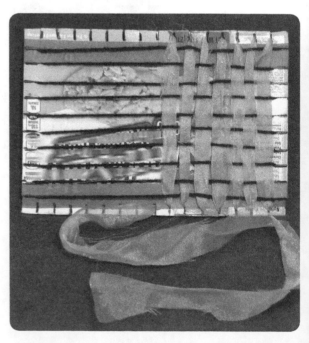

Variation:

1. Use a cracker or granola bar box to create a weaving board.
   - ▲ Remove both end tabs of the box and flatten.
   - ▲ Along all four sides, measure and mark every 0.5 in (1.3 cm).
   - ▲ At each marking, cut a 0.5-in (1.3-cm) slit.

- Create the warp or strings on the board.
  - Knot one end of the string. Insert the string in the first slit with the knot on the outside.
  - Extend the string to the slit directly across to the other side and insert it through the opposite slit.
  - Then take the string, wrap it behind the tab, and bring it through the neighboring slit.
  - Once again, bring the string across the open part of the box and into the opposite slit, around the tab, and through the neighboring slit. Continue this pattern until all slits are filled.
  - Once all slits are filled, tape the string tightly outside the last slit so that it doesn't fall back through to the inside.

- Weave
  - Knot one end of a colorful yarn. Insert the yarn in the first slit that runs perpendicular to the warp. The knot is on the outside. Thread the ribbon over and under alternating strings of the warp.
  - When the end is reached, pass the ribbon behind the tab and bring it through the neighboring slit to begin a new row.
  - Continue weaving the ribbon in the over-and-under pattern but opposite that of the previous row.
  - After finishing a row, use fingers to push the weft up next to the previous row. In the event that the weaving material runs out or if a change in material is desired halfway through, new yarn or ribbon can be tied onto the original piece and weaving can continue.

- Finish the edges of the woven piece.
  - When the piece is finished, push the tabs forward and carefully remove it from the board.
  - Starting at one end, bring the second loop under and through the first loop, pulling to secure.

- Do not drop the second loop.
  - Now move to the third loop and do the same. Bring the third loop under and through the second loop, being careful not to drop the third loop. Continue this pattern around all four sides.
  - When the second-to-last loop has passed through the last loop, make several knots so that it cannot fall back through.
  - Repeat on the opposite side of the project.

CREATIVE CASTAWAYS

Making Creative Castaways incorporates and utilizes: creativity, decision making, dexterity, hand-eye coordination, imagination, problem solving

Playing Creative Castaways utilizes: communication skills, cooperation, critical thinking, exploration of roles, imagination, perspective taking, problem solving, storytelling

Storybook castaways need food, water, and shelter. Nature provides the basics. Lucky survivors find other supplies when cargo from shipwrecks floats ashore. Then they use their heads. The Swiss Family Robinson turned empty flasks into swimming belts. Robinson Crusoe made a tent from sails. In *Hatchet*, 13-year-old Brian lights a fire by striking his small ax against flint. Using the supplies and list below, create even more "survival" items.

Supplies:

- Assorted clean, plastic recyclables
- Paper tubes
- Cardboard, tagboard, or plastic boxes of various sizes
- Plastic bottle caps
- Rubber bands
- Bits of string or yarn
- Odds and ends of various miscellaneous items (e.g., a sock, a couple wooden blocks, a clean rag, empty masking tape rounds)

Island Survival Kit Checklist

Bed	Eye patch	Megaphone
Binoculars	Fishing pole	Mousetrap
Bowl	Hat	Raft
Canteen	Knapsack	Spoon
Coconut grabber	Lantern	Tent

To Play:

- Using the assorted recyclables "collected," try to make the survival items listed in the box or others that come to mind when surveying the supplies at your disposal.

- Once the items are created, act out either a familiar story line or one that one or more people have made up.

Suggestions:

- The setting can be changed to match the stories children are reading, such as:

  ▴ Travelers in medieval times who got lost in the woods when going from one kingdom to another

  ▴ Astronauts stuck in space

  ▴ People on their own in a different culture or country

GRAPHIC NOTATION AND MUSICAL INSTRUMENTS

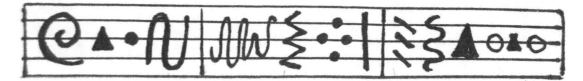

Making a Graphic Notation composition incorporates and utilizes: composition (beginning-middle-end), creativity, decision making, experimentation, expression of sense of self, hand-eye coordination, memory, part-whole relationships, problem solving, symbolic representation of sound

Playing the Graphic Notation composition utilizes: counting, creativity, experimentation with sound and rhythm, expression of emotion, expression of sense of self, grouping of sounds, interpretation of symbols

Graphic notation is a form of representing music through the use of lines, dashes, curves, dots, squiggles, etc. instead of traditional music symbols (e.g., notes, rests, key signatures, and staffs). This form of composition began in the 1950s. It allows for one to experiment with tones and rhythms without being restricted to translation of standard notation. While it provides creative freedom for those who know standard notation, it gives those who do not read music the opportunity to compose and express themselves musically (Timin, 2008).

Music notation is divided into measures, or groupings of beats. Knowing how many beats in a measure helps to know how long to play a sound. For simplicity, assume there are four beats per measure.

Supplies:

- Paper
- Markers, pen, or pencil
- Musical instruments and/or voice

To Make:

- Instructions for making a variety of instruments follow. Make and use these instruments for composing and performing the composition.

To Play:

- Try different ways to compose a song.

  ▲ Start with the paper.
    - Going from left to right, make marks across the paper. Then with an instrument, voice, and/or vocal sounds, interpret the markings.

  ▲ Start with the sounds.
    - Using voice, vocal sounds, and/or instruments (listed on the next few pages), create a melody. When complete, go to the paper and use lines and shapes to represent those sounds and their volume, duration, and sound quality.

Note: The essence of graphic notation is for the markings to be open to interpretation. However, if you'd like to develop a consistent system of musical notation, create a legend or diagram that explains what the symbols mean.

Suggestions:

- Make some of the instruments described on the following pages. Use the instruments to create and perform a composition.

- Write lyrics to the song.

Variations:

1. Exchange your composition with that of a partner. Interpret and perform one another's composition.

2. Exchange the instruments you made with those made by a partner. Create a composition and/or perform with one another's musical instrument.

3. Collaborate with a partner to create and perform a composition.

4. Organize a band or an orchestra. Practice and perform an original composition using real instruments or the homemade ones.

BALLOON BASS GUITAR

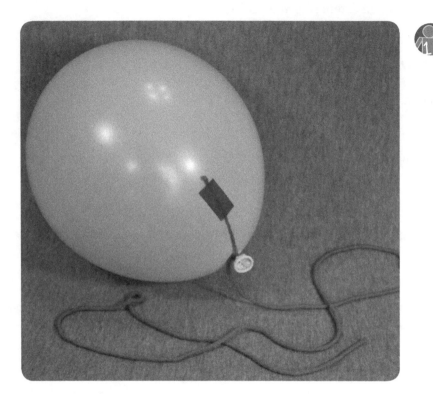

Making the Balloon Bass Guitar incorporates and utilizes: dexterity, sustained attention

Playing the Balloon Bass Guitar utilizes: hand-eye coordination, listening, music fundamentals (duration, pitch, rhythm, **timbre**), problem solving, science of sound

Supplies:

- Latex balloon, 9–11 in (22.9–27.9 cm) in size
- 2 ft (61 cm) of string or yarn
- Tape

To Make:

- Inflate the balloon.

- Tie a knot at the end.

- Tie the string to the balloon's knot so that one end of the string is 3 in (7.6 cm) long.

- While making sure the 3-in (7.6-cm) end of string is taut, tape it to the side of the balloon.

To Play:

- Hold the balloon under one arm and the longer section of string with the other hand.

- Stretch out the string so it is taut.

- Pluck the string with the hand of the arm that has the balloon.

- Create a musical composition.

Suggestions:

- Experiment with the tautness of the string to create different pitches.

  ▲ What is the relationship between tautness and pitch?

- Figure out how to play a familiar tune such as "Twinkle, Twinkle, Little Star."

BALLOON BASS GUITAR

BOX HARP

Making the Box Harp incorporates and utilizes: decision making, dexterity, hand-eye coordination, listening, sequencing

Playing the Box Harp utilizes: fine motor skills, hand-eye coordination, listening, music fundamentals (duration, pitch, rhythm, timbre), problem solving, science of sound

Supplies:

- Tissue box or shoebox with lid
- 5 to 8 rubber bands, 2 to 4 in (5.1 to 10.2 cm) in length and different widths
- Scissors

To Make:

- If needed, enlarge the opening in the top of tissue box, or cut an opening in a shoebox lid. Do not remove the entire top of the box.

- Stretch rubber bands around the width of the box.

To Play:

- With your index finger, pluck the rubber bands to create sounds.

- Create a musical composition.

Suggestions:

- Experiment with different widths and lengths of rubber bands and their tautness to achieve sounds of different pitch and timbre. Arrange them from highest to lowest pitch.

  ▲ Do wider rubber bands produce the same sound as thinner ones of the same length?

  ▲ What is the relationship between tautness and pitch?

- Figure out how to play a familiar tune such as "Twinkle, Twinkle, Little Star."

BOX HARP

BUZZY HARMONICA

Making the Buzzy Harmonica incorporates and utilizes: dexterity, following directions, hand-eye coordination, sustained attention

Playing the Buzzy Harmonica utilizes: music fundamentals (duration, rhythm, timbre), problem solving, science of sound

Supplies:

- 2 wooden craft sticks, 0.75 in (1.9 cm) wide
- 1 wide rubber band [approximately 0.25 in (0.6 cm) wide and 3 in (7.6 cm) long (not stretched)]
- 2 smaller rubber bands [approximately .06 in (0.2 cm) wide]
- 2 strips of paper, 0.75 in x 4 in (1.9 cm x 10.2 cm)
- Tape

To Make:

- Put the two craft sticks together like a sandwich. Wrap the strips of paper completely around each end of the "stick sandwich." Secure the ends of the paper with a piece of tape, making sure the tape does not adhere to the sticks.

- Slide out one of the sticks, keeping the paper in place on the other one. Carefully set the stick with the paper on the table.

- On the empty stick, stretch the wide rubber band lengthwise from end to end. Carefully place the stick with the rubber band on top of the stick with the paper. <u>Do not</u> put the rubber band stick inside the paper.

- Wrap a small rubber band around both sticks at each end.

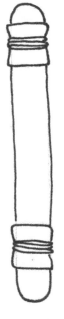
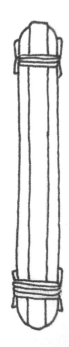

To Play:

- Blow air through the small space between the sticks.

Suggestions:

- Experiment with the amount of airflow to change pitches.

- Try pinching the ends while blowing. Why might this result in a different sound?

BUZZY HARMONICA

DRUMS

Making the Drums incorporates and utilizes: creativity, estimation, fine motor skills

Playing the Drums utilizes: counting, gross motor skills, hand-eye coordination, music fundamentals (duration, rhythm, timbre)

Supplies:

- Oatmeal tub, plastic ice cream tub, shortening tub, etc. with lids
- Two chopsticks or sticks from outside
- Yarn or other thick string, approximately 3 ft (91.4 cm)
- Hole punch

To Make:

- Remove the lid from the tub and set it aside for later. Using a hole punch, make two holes in the tub walls, opposite one another and approximately 3 in (7.6 cm) below the rim.

- Tie a big knot at the end of the piece of yarn. String it <u>from the inside of the tub</u> through one hole. The yarn should not come all the way through the hole but catch at the knot.

- The unknotted end should now be outside the tub. String it <u>from the outside of the tub</u> into the other hole. The untied end should now be inside the tub. Tie a knot in this end to keep the yarn from coming back out of the tub. Note: If the hole is too big and the yarn comes through, tie one or two more knots on top of the one that was already tied to make the knot bigger.

- Replace the lid on the tub, being sure to keep the yarn outside. Place the yarn over one shoulder and your head so that the drum hangs in front of the body, slightly to one side.

To Play:

- Use the chopsticks or tree sticks to play the drum.

Suggestions:

- Experiment with different rhythms, speeds, and strengths with which the sticks hit the drum.
  - Is it easier to keep rhythm with the dominant hand?
  - Does the side of the body on which the drum hangs make a difference in how well it can be played?
  - Is it better to play sitting or standing?

Variations:

1. Tin cans, especially in a variety of sizes, can make a very nice drum set. Make sure that any can used is free of sharp edges. Simply turn the can over and drum on the bottom. For a large drum, coffee tins work great, as well as other bulk food item tins, such as bulk canned vegetables or fruit. For smaller drums, try smaller coffee tins, 32-oz (946.4-mL) cans from tomato sauce, and 16-oz (473.2-mL) cans from beans, veggies, fruit, sauces, etc. Want a tiny drum? Add a small tin that once held breath mints!

2. To decorate the drum set, find tissue paper of various colors used in gift bags or boxes. Cut the tissue into small squares or other shapes. Dip entire pieces of cut tissue into glue (white or rubber cement will work), and plaster onto the tins. Once all the desired tissue is in place, set aside to dry completely.

DRUMS

KAZOO

Making the Kazoo incorporates and utilizes: creativity, dexterity

Playing the Kazoo utilizes: breath control, listening, music fundamentals (duration, pitch, rhythm, timbre)

Supplies:

- Paper tube, 4–6 inches (10.2–15.2 cm) in length
- Wax paper cut into a 4-in x 4-in (10.2-cm x 10.2-cm) square
- Rubber band
- Hole punch

To Make:

- With the hole punch, begin by making a hole in one end of the paper tube, approximately 2 in (5.1 cm) from the end.

- Place the 4-in (10.2-cm) square of wax paper on top of the opening at the end of the paper tube near the hole punch. Making sure the wax paper is pulled taut, wrap the excess down along the length of the tube with one hand. Secure the wax paper in place with the rubber band, doubling the band if it is too loose. The tube should now be closed off on one end, but make sure the punched hole isn't covered.

- Make sure the wax paper is completely sealed with the rubber band.

To Play:

- Place the open end of the kazoo to the mouth and hum or sing into it.

KAZOO

ROCKIN' CEREAL BOX GUITAR

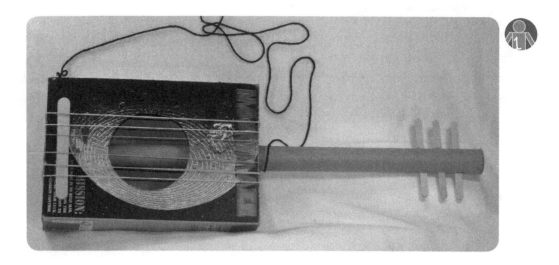

Making the Rockin' Cereal Box Guitar incorporates and utilizes: concentration, dexterity, fine-motor skills, following directions, hand-eye coordination, listening, measurement, patience, sequencing, spatial relations, sustained attention

Playing the Rockin' Cereal Box Guitar utilizes: concentration, expression of sense of self, fine motor skills, imagination, listening, music fundamentals (pitch, rhythm, timbre), problem solving, science of sound

Supplies:

- Cereal box with top and bottom tabs undone
- Long paper tube (wrapping paper tube), approximately 30 inches (76.2 cm) in length
- 3 wooden craft sticks, 0.4 in (1 cm) wide
- Large wooden craft stick, 0.75 in (1.9 cm) wide
- 6 rubber bands, 5–9 in (12.7–22.9 cm) in length, different widths
- Yarn or ribbon, 3–4 ft (91.4 to 121.9 cm)
- Pencil
- Scissors
- Hole punch
- Tape
- Toothpick
- Ruler
- Compass (optional)
- Glue (optional)

To Make:

- Lay the flattened cereal box on the table with the front of the box facing up, the top of the box away, and a side panel on the right hand side. In the lower right-hand corner (not including the tabs), approximately 0.5 in (1.3 cm) above the fold, punch a hole through both layers. (This is where the guitar strap will be attached later on.) Return the box to the original 3-dimensional shape and tape or glue both ends. (Note: If using glue, allow time for it to dry.)

- To create the sound hole, cut a large circle/square [no more than 4 in (10.2 cm) in diameter] in the front face of the box. The opening should not come within 2 in (5.1 cm) of the sides of the box.

- Find the midpoint on the bottom and top sides of the box. Starting at the midpoint, draw a circle with the same radius as that of the paper tube. Cut out the circles; these are the openings for the neck of the guitar.

- Insert the tube through the box so that both ends of the tube are sticking out. Starting with the tube at the bottom of the box, cut eight evenly spaced 0.75-inch- (1.9-cm-) long slits into the tube. Fan out, or spread, the "fingers" of the cut tube; adhere each one to the box. (If using glue, allow for it to dry.) On the other end of the cereal box, apply strips of tape to secure the neck (tube) in place.

- Stretch the rubber bands lengthwise around the cereal box. Arrange them so that they are over the opening and not touching one another. At 1–2 in (2.5–5.1 cm) below the sound hole, slide the large wooden craft stick under the rubber bands to form the bridge.

  ▲ Pluck the rubber bands to hear their pitch. Arrange the rubber bands from lowest to highest pitch.

- Tuning pegs on a real guitar are located on the sides of the neck. They hold one end of the guitar's strings. Turning the pegs tightens and loosens the strings, which changes their pitch. To simulate tuning pegs, craft sticks are inserted toward the end of the paper tube. On both the left side and the right side of the neck (tube), measure 3 in (7.6 cm) from the end. At the 3-in (7.6-cm), 2-in (5.1-cm), and 1-in (2.5-cm) marks, make a 0.5-in (1.3-cm) slit lengthwise. You will have made six slits total: three on one side and three directly opposite. Slide a smaller craft stick through each of the pairs of slits.

ROCKIN' CEREAL BOX GUITAR

▲ Hint: To determine the sides of the neck, set the box flat on the table with the neck pointing away. From this position, the left side of the box and tube are on the left; the right side of the box and tube are on the right.

- To attach the strap, tape one end of the yarn (or ribbon) to one end of a toothpick using a piece of tape. Thread the toothpick through the holes punched at the start of this process. Remove the yarn from the toothpick, and tie a knot. Take the other end of the yarn and tie it around the neck where it attaches to the body of the guitar. Tape into place.

To Play:

Holding the guitar

- Sit on a chair and put the guitar on your lap with the sound hole to the outside.
  - ▲ If your right hand is your dominant hand, the neck goes on the left.
  - ▲ If your left hand is your dominant hand, the neck goes on the right.
- Put the guitar strap over your neck.
  - ▲ If your right hand is your dominant hand, put the guitar strap behind your right shoulder and arm.
  - ▲ If your left hand is your dominant hand, put the guitar strap behind your left shoulder and arm.

Playing the guitar

- Pluck the rubber bands with the index finger of your dominant hand.
- Strum the rubber bands with the thumb on your dominant hand.
- Strum from the top down and from the bottom up.

Suggestions:

- Note: Changing the craft sticks from a flat to perpendicular position increases the tension on the rubber bands, which changes the pitch and timbre.
  - ▲ Is there a relationship between tautness and pitch?
- Is the sound different strumming from top down than strumming from bottom up?
- Experiment with different widths and lengths of rubber bands and their tautness to achieve sounds of different pitch and timbre.
  - ▲ Do wider rubber bands produce the same sound as thinner ones of the same length?
- Figure out how to play a familiar tune such as "Twinkle, Twinkle, Little Star."
- Create a musical composition.

SHAKERS

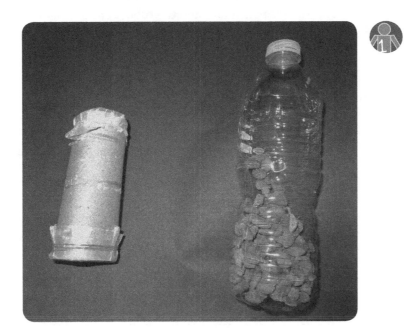

Making the Shakers incorporates and utilizes: creativity, dexterity, measurement

Playing the Shakers utilizes: counting, gross motor skills, music fundamentals (duration, rhythm, timbre), problem solving

Supplies:

- Paper tube, 4–6 inches (10.2–15.2 cm)
- 2 pieces of wax paper, approximately a 4-in (10.2-cm) square
- 2 medium-sized rubber bands
- Handful of clean pebbles

To Make:

- Begin by placing one 4-in (10.2-cm) square of wax paper on top of one opening at the end of the paper tube. Making sure the wax paper is pulled taut, wrap the excess down along the length of the tube with one hand. Secure the wax paper in place with one rubber band, doubling the band if it is too loose. The tube should now be closed off on one end.

- Place the tube on a flat surface with the open end facing up. Place the handful of pebbles into the tube.

- Now, cover the open end with the other piece of wax paper and rubber band, again, making sure the wax paper is pulled taut and the rubber band is tight.

- To make sure that the pebbles are secure, perform a few test shakes.

  ▲ Begin by shaking gently and get more vigorous with each new shake. If the shaker can be used with rapid, relatively forceful motions, it is ready to go.

  ▲ If a test shake results in one of the wax paper pieces falling off, replace it, but try using a slightly smaller rubber band, or wrapping the current band three times around the tube.

To Play:

- Shake back and forth or up and down to a particular rhythm.

- Try rolling the shaker across the floor for a different sound.

Suggestions:

- Does the shaker sound change depending on how many pebbles are in it?

- What does the shaker sound like if scrap paper is used instead of wax paper? What other items could be used to cover the ends of the shaker?

- What else could go inside the shaker, besides pebbles? How does the sound change if other materials are used?

Variation:

1. For a simpler shaker, use a water or juice bottle with its lid. Remove the lid and place pebbles inside. For smaller bottle openings, a funnel can be easily made by rolling a piece of newspaper or scrap paper and placing about 2 in (5.1 cm) of the roll inside the bottle mouth. Let go of the paper roll and the top will unfurl, making a funnel. Pebbles can now be more easily poured into the bottle. Make sure they are small enough to fit through the funnel. Clean aquarium gravel works very well for this. Once pebbles are inside, replace and secure the bottle lid and shake.

STRAW PAN FLUTE

Making the Straw Pan Flute incorporates and utilizes: experimentation of length and pitch, focus, hand-eye coordination, measurement, patience, sequencing

Playing the Straw Pan Flute utilizes: breath control, listening, musical creativity, music fundamentals (duration, pitch, rhythm, timbre), science of sound

Supplies:

- 8 to 10 plastic drinking straws
  - ▲ Nonbending are ideal, but bending ones can be used
  - ▲ Opening should be at least 0.25 in (0.6 cm) in diameter (Note: bubble tea straws work best)
- Ruler
- Scissors
- Masking tape or painter's tape
- Fine point marker (optional)

To Make:

If the drinking straws have a bend, remove them by cutting directly below and above the bend. Use the longer pieces for the directions below. Use the shorter cuttings as the spacers.

- Straw 1: Seal one end of the straw with tape. Set it aside.

- Straw 2: Cut 0.5 in (1.3 cm) of length.
  - ▲ Discard the 0.5-in (1.3-cm) cutting.
  - ▲ Seal one end of the remaining straw with tape and set aside.

- Straw 3: Cut 1 in (2.5 cm) of length.
  - ▲ Save the 1-inch (2.5-cm) segment to use as a spacer.
  - ▲ Seal one end of the remaining straw with tape and set aside.

- Straw 4: Cut 1.5 in (3.8 cm) of length.
  - ▲ Cut 0.5 in (1.3 cm) from the 1.5-in (3.8-cm) segment and save to use as a spacer.
  - ▲ Discard the 0.5-inch (1.3-cm) piece.
  - ▲ Seal one end of the remaining straw with tape and set aside.

- Straw 5: Cut 2 in (5.1 cm) of length.
  - ▲ Save the 2-in (5.1-cm) segment to use as a spacer.
  - ▲ Seal one end of the remaining straw with tape and set aside.

- Straw 6: Cut 2.5 in (6.4 cm) of length.
  - ▲ Cut 0.5 in (1.3 cm) from the 2.5-in (6.4-cm) segment. Save the 2-in (5.1-cm) segment to use as a spacer and discard the 0.5-in (1.3-cm) cutting.
  - ▲ Seal one end of the remaining straw with tape and set aside.

- Straw 7: Cut 3 in (7.6 cm) of length.
  - ▲ Cut 1 in (2.5 cm) from the 3-in (7.6-cm) segment. Save the 2-in (5.1-cm) segment to use as a spacer and discard the 1-in (2.5-cm) cutting.
  - ▲ Seal one end of the remaining straw with tape and set aside.

- Straw 8: Cut 3.5 in (8.9 cm) of length.
  - ▲ Cut 1.5 in (3.8 cm) from the 3.5-in (8.9-cm) segment. Save the 2-in (5.1-cm) piece to use as a spacer and discard the 1.5-in (3.8-cm) cutting.
  - ▲ Seal one end of the remaining straw with tape and set aside.

Spacers

- If the straws being used do not have bends, create 2-in (5.1-cm) spacers from the remaining straws. A total of nine spacers are needed.

Assemble

- On a flat surface, lay an 11-in (27.9-cm) piece of tape with the sticky side up. Curl each end under a bit so that it sticks to the surface. (Curling it under aids in keeping the tape in place.)

- The first piece to go on the tape is a spacer. This is one of the short pieces of straw that is not sealed off with tape. Place a spacer at one end on top of the tape, making sure that the spacer's end is in alignment with the upper edge of the tape.

- Directly next to this spacer goes Straw 1. Place this straw with the open end 0.5 in (1.3 cm) above the tape edge.

- Next to Straw 1 is a spacer. As with the first spacer, align one end with the upper edge of the tape.

- Repeat the sequencing of spacer-straw, making sure that the tops of the spacers align with the upper edge of the tape and that all the open ends of the sealed straws are aligned with one another and are 0.5 inch (1.3 cm) above the tape line.

- Once all nine spacers and eight straws are in place, undo the tape from the surface and wrap it around the straws, making sure it wraps entirely around both sides.
  - ▲ Be careful not to wrap too tightly. The pan flute is to remain flat.

To Play:

- Blow air across and down the open ends of the sealed-off straws.

- Hint: Simulate playing a flute.

Suggestions:

- Use straws with larger/smaller diameters.

- Use different lengths of straws. For example, instead of decreasing the length of each straw by 0.5 in (1.3 cm), decrease each by 0.25 in (0.6 cm) or 0.75 in (1.9 cm). Are the pitches different?

Note: For more information about this activity, such as scientific information and mathematical calculations on length of straws and pitch, run an online search for "straw pan flute."

STRAW PAN FLUTE

TWEETER

Making the Tweeter incorporates and utilizes: angles, fine motor skills, measurement

Playing the Tweeter utilizes: breath control, experimentation, patience, science of sound

Supplies:

- Plastic drinking straw, preferably 0.25 in (0.6 cm) in diameter
- Ruler
- Marker
- Scissors

To Make:

- Cut one end of the straw to create a point with a 45-degree angle. To do this, measure the diameter of the straw's opening.

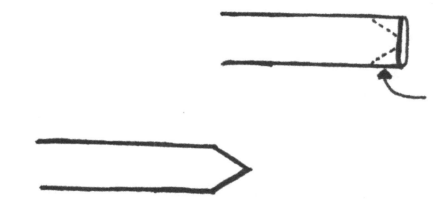

- Press down one end of the straw. Starting at that end, measure and mark down the length of the straw a distance equal to the straw's diameter. For example, if the straw has an opening diameter of 0.25 in (0.6 cm), then measure down the length of the straw 0.25 inch (0.6 cm) and mark.

- Make two cuts from the midpoint of the straw's opening to the marked length. One cut will angle to the right and the other cut will angle to the left.

To Play:

- Slightly curl your lips under and place them on the straw's pointed opening. Press down slightly with your lips and blow. It may take a number of attempts at playing before creating a sound.

- With each attempt, change the position of your lips on the straw, the pressure of your lips on the straw, and the effort in blowing. Think of how musicians play the double-reed instruments (e.g., oboe, English horn, bassoon).

Suggestions:

- Make additional tweeters using drinking straws of larger or smaller diameters. Is the range of pitch the same using straws of the same length but different diameters?

- Want to modify the sound? Insert and tape the end of the straw through a hole in the bottom of a yogurt cup.

TWEETER

LOOK AND FIND

Making Look and Find incorporates and utilizes: creativity, decision making, planning

Playing Look and Find utilizes: cooperation, emotional regulation, imagination, perseverance, sustained attention

Supplies:

- Pillowcase
- Clear plastic vinyl (or packaging from bedding)
- Duct tape
- Packing peanuts
- Paper
- Pencil
- Scissors
- **Trinkets**
  - ▲ Small plastic animals
  - ▲ Game board pieces
  - ▲ Colored balls

To Make:

- Begin by creating a list on a sheet of paper of the items that are to be found (trinkets) so the children know what they are looking for.

- Cut a square hole in a pillowcase.

- Cut out a piece of clear plastic vinyl (for example, packaging from bedding) that will overlap the square hole in the pillowcase.

- Using the duct tape, attach the clear plastic vinyl to the inside of the pillowcase so that it completely covers the square opening.

- Fill the pillowcase with packing peanuts.

- Add some trinkets and items to find.

- Tape the pillowcase shut.

- To create another Look and Find game, plastic bedding packaging (uncut) can be reused by simply unzipping, filling with packing peanuts and trinkets, and zipping back up.

To Play:

- Each child creates his or her own look-and-find game (great for long car or bus rides). Children can switch games with one another and find the items on each other's lists.

- The player shakes the bag until one of the lost items comes into view, allowing him or her to cross it off the list. Play ends when the player finds all items.

Suggestions:

- Instead of a pillowcase, use a clear pencil bag or plastic bottle. Fill the bag or bottle with filler (shredded paper) and trinkets, put the lid on, and tape it closed.

- Players can take turns telling a story based on the items they find in the bag or bottle. As the player finds another object, he or she has to incorporate that item into the plot of the story.

- Create bags with different themes. For example, only include trinkets or small objects that meet these requirements:
  - ▲ Items that start with the letter "B" (miniature baseball, bottle caps, bracelet)
  - ▲ Items that could be found in a classroom (eraser, pencil, glue stick)
  - ▲ Trinkets that represent your favorite things (food, clothes, movies)

PUPPET

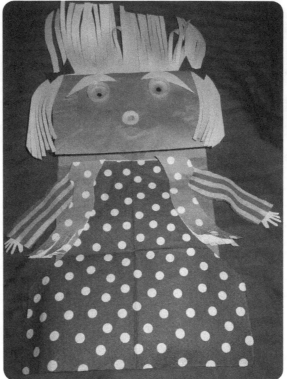

Making the Puppet incorporates and utilizes: creativity, decision making, dexterity, expression of sense of self, hand-eye coordination, imagination, reading comprehension (if creating a story character), spatial relations

Playing with the Puppet utilizes: character understanding (if creating a story character), communication skills, creativity, emotion exploration, exploration of sense of self, imagination, language, role exploration, role-playing, social relations, storytelling skills

Supplies:

- Paper lunch bag
- Yarn scraps
- Fabric bits
- Old newspapers or magazines
- Construction paper scraps

>Supplies continued

- Other extra scraps (cotton, string, packing materials, glitter, etc.)
- Markers, crayons, or colored pencils
- Glue or tape
- Scissors

To Make:

- Begin by placing the closed paper bag on the table with the bottom flap facing up. Slide a hand into the opening of the bag with fingers reaching into the bottom flap. Moving the fingers up and down should make the flap of the bag move away from and toward the rest of the bag. This is how the puppet's mouth will work when finished.

- The puppet can now be decorated using creativity and imagination. Decide where the nose goes, where the eyes go, etc. Will it have arms? Legs? Will it be a person or an animal? An alien? A monster? Will it be something completely new that can be created and named?

To Play:

- Puppets may be used in solitary play to exercise individual imagination or in groups to explore relationships. Consider the suggestions below.

Suggestions:

- What attributes does the puppet share with the puppet master? What attributes might it have that the puppet master lacks?

- How might the puppet interact with another puppet?

- If one puppet is a bunny and another puppet is a dog, how would they play together?

- Is the puppet a character in a story players have read? What part of the story can be acted out with the puppet?

- Use the puppets as a tool to help students create, write down, and then act out a brand new story.

PUPPET

STORY CARDS

Playing Story Cards utilizes: abstract thinking, character creation, character vs. narrator roles, creativity, decision making, establishment of plot, imagination, setting creation and description, story line development (beginning, middle, end)

Supplies:

- At least 24 fronts of various greeting cards and/or postcards that have pictures or artwork

To Play:

- Place greeting cards facedown in a pile.
- Select any three cards.
- Incorporate elements on those cards into a story, poem, fable, or myth.

Variation:

1. Play cooperatively: The first player turns over a card and is allowed to tell three sentences of a story based on the images from that card. The second player then flips over another card and has to <u>continue</u> the same story by incorporating elements from the new card. Play continues until cards run out or the story reaches a natural end.

TANGRAMS

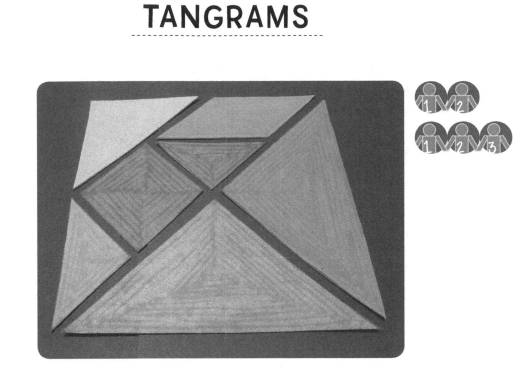

Making Tangrams incorporates and utilizes: dextcrity, hand eyc coordination, measurement, part-whole relationships, understanding of shapes and geometrical terms (e.g., parallel)

Playing with Tangrams utilizes: decision making, geometry, part-whole relationships, persistence, spatial relations

Supplies:

- Front of a large cereal box OR a large piece of tagboard
- Ruler
- Pencil
- Scissors
- Crayons or markers

To Make:

- Measure the shorter side of the tagboard and cut the longer side to make a square. [If the tagboard is 8 in x 12 in (20.3 cm x 30.5 cm), trim the 12-in (30.5-cm) side to 8 in (20.3 cm).]

- On the plain side of the board, use a ruler to draw a line from the bottom left corner of the square to the top right corner, making two large triangles.

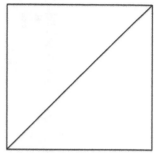

- Measure to find the length of 0.75 of this line. This will be the length of your next line. Place your ruler so that it runs from the bottom right corner of the square to the top left corner. Starting at the bottom right corner, draw a line the length that you just found. You should now see an "X" on your board with a bit of the top left side missing.

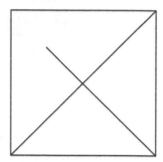

- Next, draw a line parallel to the line running across the square from bottom left to top right that <u>goes through the end of the other diagonal line</u>. You can do this by placing the ruler at the end of the incomplete diagonal line and eyeballing when the ruler is parallel to the first diagonal. Or you can measure the length from the center of your square to the end of the incomplete diagonal and make one dot the same length away to the left of it and one to the right. Then simply use your ruler to connect the dots.

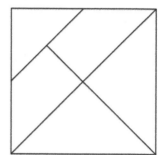

- Now, draw a line from the point where this new line meets the left edge of your board to the first diagonal. This line should be parallel to the incomplete diagonal. You will now see a triangle and square in that small strip.

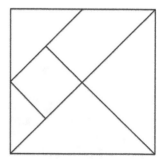

- Lastly, draw a line from where the incomplete diagonal meets the top line to the first diagonal line. This new line should be parallel to the top edge of your board. You will now see a new triangle and a parallelogram.

- Darken the lines drawn on the board, and color or draw on the shapes if desired.

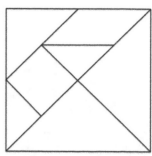

- Cut out all the pieces. (There should be seven.)

To Play:

- The simplest way to play this game is to mix up the pieces and then attempt to put them back into a square.

- Allow some time to pass between creating the game and playing so players forget how they made the pieces from the square.

- Competition may be brought in by having a race to see who can make a square the first.

Suggestions:

- How can the smaller shapes be combined into something different from a square? (Each shape must use more than one piece.)
  - ▲ A giant triangle?
  - ▲ A smaller square?
  - ▲ Two squares?

- Placing the pieces on a sheet of scrap paper, create a new shape. Trace the outline of this shape and remove the tangrams. Trade with a partner and try to re-create the other person's shape.

- Do an online search for "tangram silhouettes," choose an image, and compete to see who can make the picture first.

TANGRAMS

CHAPTER 5
Links and Chains

Dad: *Did you know there is a number between 3 and 4 called pi?*

Son: *No, there isn't. It goes 3 then 4.*

Dad: *But there is a number in between called pi. It is 3.14.*

Son: *3.14?*

Dad: *Yes.*

Son: *So when I count I should say "One, two, three, pie, four, five"?*

Sometimes fun can be found in otherwise complex and/or frustrating situations. The English language can fit that bill easily, especially for new learners, young and old. But just as much as we can get frustrated learning about words and numbers, we can play with them and the concepts surrounding them. Games and activities in this chapter focus on skills relating to sequencing, making connections between and among words and numbers, and spatial relationships.

Games in This Chapter:

- **CapWords:** Engage in tactile wordplay with just a few recycled materials.

- **Fishing Match:** Catch and release sea creatures to build number sense.

- **Get the Picture?:** Compare and contrast images using geometric shapes.

- **It's in the Bag:** Sort and match symbols and words with a version of an Inuit game.

- **Jianzi:** Construct a shuttlecock to strengthen agility and counting skills.

- **Order Up!:** Find items in this memory game and put them in the correct order to win.

- **Play Money:** Practice making change and improve saving skills with this easily created play currency.

- **Rock-n-Roll Math:** Rock out combinations of numbers with the roll of the dice.

- **Shape Toss:** Use gross-motor tossing skills to identify shapes and colors.

- **Similarities:** Identify commonalities among random images.

- **Up and Down the Number Line:** Create a hopscotch-like game to practice counting and other math skills.

CAPWORDS

Making CapWords incorporates and utilizes: dexterity, letter-learning, literacy, planning

Playing CapWords utilizes: competition, decision-making, dexterity, literacy (e.g., spelling, vocabulary, word recognition), selective attention, sustained attention

Supplies:

- 100 plastic caps from 12–16-oz (354.9–473.2-mL) water bottles (preferably the same color)
- 10 pieces of string, 24 in (61 cm) long (more if needed)
- Permanent marker
- Pen
- Ruler
- 17-in x 20-in (43.2-cm x 50.8-cm) sheet of easel paper or recycled paper

To Make:

- Each bottle cap will have one letter written on the top of it in permanent marker. The breakdown of letters is as follows:

A: 9 caps	H: 2 caps	O: 8 caps	V: 2 caps
B: 2 caps	I: 9 caps	P: 2 caps	W: 2 caps
C: 2 caps	J: 1 cap	Q: 1 cap	X: 1 cap
D: 4 caps	K: 1 cap	R: 6 caps	Y: 3 caps
E: 12 caps	L: 4 caps	S: 4 caps	Z: 1 cap
F: 2 caps	M: 3 caps	T: 6 caps	
G: 3 caps	N: 6 caps	U: 4 caps	

To Play:

- Using the ruler and pen, begin by drawing a grid that is 15 in x 15 in (38.1 cm x 38.1 cm) on the large sheet of paper. The grid should be 10 squares x 10 squares, with each square measuring 1.5 in (3.8 cm).

- Make a list of desired words and, using the letters on the caps, fit them into the grid:
  - ▲ Only one cap can be placed in each box.
  - ▲ Remember that each new word can be placed independently or can build off of another word. For example, if the word "playful" is already on the grid, "learning" can be placed across it by using the same letter "A" cap.
  - ▲ Words may be placed vertically, horizontally, or diagonally. For more advanced players, words may orient forward or backward.

- When all words are placed, fill in the remaining squares with the rest of the caps.

- The puzzle solver now searches for the words using the list the creator made. When the solver finds a word, he or she will circle it by placing one string around it. The game ends when the solver finds all the words or gives up.

Suggestions:

- This is a great activity for spelling lessons.
- This can be used to familiarize students with vocabulary from various subjects.
- Create a number version in which students must find the sum, difference, product, and/ or quotient of problems.

Variation:

1. Create a crossword: If caps are see through, place them in a bag and have each player choose seven caps. If caps are opaque, they can be turned upside down and placed to the side of the playing surface. Players take turns making words from their caps, with each new word connecting to the existing board. Note: The string is not necessary in this version, as the "finding" happens mentally before caps are placed on the board.

FISHING MATCH

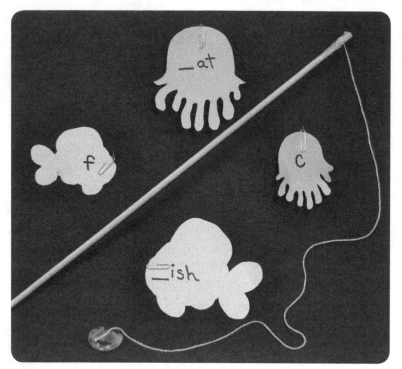

Making Fishing Match incorporates and utilizes: colors, dexterity, hand-eye coordination, knowledge of aquatic life, shapes, symbols and meaning

Playing Fishing Match utilizes: colors, cooperation skills, decision making, dexterity, emergent literacy, hand-eye coordination, selective attention, shapes, symbols and meaning, turn taking

Supplies:

- 5 to 6 used file folders
- Paper clips
- Stick or wooden dowel rod, 2 ft (61 cm) long
  - ▲ Cardboard tubing from a trouser hanger can also be used, though it is shorter
- String, 3 ft (91.4 cm)
- Magnet strong enough to lift a paper clip and 4-in (10.2-cm) square piece of cardstock
- Scissors
- Markers
- Blue towel or cloth (optional)

This game requires creating both a fishing pole and fish.

To Make:

Fishing pole

- Tie one end of the string to the tip of the stick or wooden dowel rod. On the other end of the string, tie or tape a magnet that will be strong enough to pick up the fish.

Fish

- Draw and cut fish shapes from the used file folders. The fish should be 4–5 in (10.2–12.7 cm) long.
- Slide a paper clip on the nose of the fish.

Make at least 20 fish—10 fish per set. Determine the basis for matching. For example, if it is numerals and amounts, write numerals on one set of fish (one numeral per fish) and dots corresponding to the amounts on the other set. Note: Be sure to write on BOTH sides of the fish. For letter recognition, write uppercase letters on one set of fish and the corresponding lowercase letters on the other set. Or for number word recognition, write the numerals on the first set of fish and the number words on the other set.

To Play:

- Lay the blue towel on the floor. This is the sea.
- Arrange all the fish in the sea.
- Using the fishing pole, lower the magnet to the targeted fish.
- Once connected, raise the pole and remove the fish.
- Find and catch the mate to that fish.

FISHING MATCH

Suggestions:

- If different colors of file folders are available, use one color for one set of fish and another color for the other set.

- Create different types of sea animals for each category. For example, have the numeral on a fish shape, the English number word on an octopus shape, and the Spanish number word on a turtle.

- Introduce memory skills: Using the same color folders, write the numerals on only ONE side of one set and the English number words on only ONE side of the other set of fish. Place fish so the blank sides face up. Players try to find the corresponding fish. If they find a match, they keep that set. If there is no match, fish must be returned to their previous position in the sea.

Variation:

1. Play this game with others to determine the best **angler** amongst your friends.

GET THE PICTURE?

Playing Get the Picture utilizes: abstract thinking, communication skills, concentration, critical thinking, decision making, geometry (e.g., angles, symmetry), perceptual skills (positive/negative space), problem solving, selective attention, spatial relations, vocabulary

Supplies:

- At least one dozen fronts of various greeting cards and/or postcards that have pictures or artwork

To Play:

- Place greeting cards facedown in a pile.

- Select a card. Carefully study it. Identify and talk about the images on the card—for example, geometric shapes, positive and negative space, symmetry, angles, parallel lines, and/or horizontal, vertical, and diagonal lines.

- Once the features have been identified, place the card back in the pile, shuffle the cards, and select another one.

Variations:

1. Place cards facedown in a pile. The first player selects a card and points out one geometric or spatial characteristic. The next player selects the next card in the pile and looks for the same characteristic. If it cannot be found, that card is placed in a discard pile and another card is drawn.

2. Place cards facedown in a pile. The first player selects a card and points out one geometric or spatial characteristic. The next player must find the same geometric or spatial characteristic in the room.

IT'S IN THE BAG

This activity is inspired by the Inuit game Inukat, a game that tests one's knowledge of seal anatomy, ability to differentiate shapes, and quickness of hands. For the original game, each player is given a bag of mixed bones. Most of the bones are from the hind flipper fin of a seal. However, there are also other seal bones as well as bones from other animals. On cue, each player empties the contents of his or her bag onto the table and reconstructs the fin to the best of his or her ability (Inuit Bone Gambling Game and Puzzle, 2010). We have listed four versions of this game. Our versions test participants' knowledge of geometric shapes, vocabulary, parts of speech, spatial abilities, and categorization skills. Specific skills utilized are listed before each version's instructions.

Note: This game requires both a drawstring bag and game pieces. The supply list below is for all four versions of the game.

Supplies:

- Drawstring bag or paper bag
  - ▲ Clean T-shirt (men's XL)
  - ▲ 2 pieces of string or yarn, each 12 in (30.5 cm) long
  - ▲ Fabric tape, fabric glue, or needle and thread
  - ▲ Small safety pin
  - ▲ Scissors
- 2 cereal boxes or other tagboard
- 30 or 70 plastic caps from plastic jugs
  - ▲ If 30 caps: 10 of one color, 20 of a second color
  - ▲ If 70 caps: 10 of one color, 10 of a second color, 10 of a third color, and 40 of a fourth color
- Paper
- Pencil or waterproof pen
- Compass
- Straightedge or ruler
- Craft or tacky glue
- Scissors

To Make:

Make the drawstring bag.

- At the shoulder seam, cut each sleeve from the T-shirt. (Save the T-shirt and use to make a knapsack another day.)

- Turn the sleeve inside out so that the right sides of the fabric are touching. Join the two sides of the fabric at the seamed (shoulder) end by using fabric tape, fabric glue, or by sewing them together. (If using fabric tape or fabric glue, follow the directions on the package.)

- To create the opening for the drawstring, make a small cut on both sides of the side seam at the cuff end, making sure that <u>only one thickness</u> of fabric is cut.

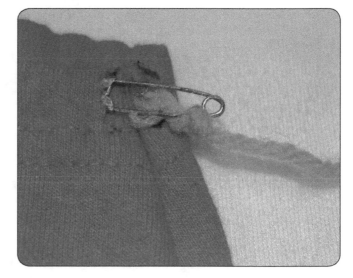

- Take one of the pieces of string, tie a knot at one end, and attach the safety pin through the knot. Insert the head of the safety pin in the slit. Using your fingers, maneuver the safety pin around the circumference and out through the other opening.

- Remove the safety pin. Tie the two ends of the string together.

Prepare plastic cap game pieces.

- Using the compass, calculate the circumference of the inner circle/opening of the cap. This is the measurement you will use to make circles on sheets of paper.

- Test the measurement by cutting one of the circles and laying it inside the plastic cap. If it fits nicely, continue on drawing circles. If it doesn't fit, adjust measurements accordingly.

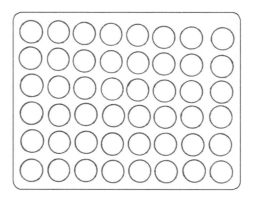

- Make 30 or 70 circles, depending on how many caps you are using. Write a number or word inside each circle. Note: The number or word written will depend on the game you choose to play. (Suggestions follow.)

- Once all the numbers or words are written, carefully cut around each circle and, using craft glue, fasten the paper circle inside the cap. Allow caps to dry. When caps are dry, store them in a paper bag or drawstring bag.

Suggestions and Variations:

VERSION 1:
Number-Word Matching

Making It's in the Bag: Number-Word Matching incorporates and utilizes:
dexterity, hand-eye coordination, literacy, measurement, number sense, writing

Playing It's in the Bag: Number-Word Matching utilizes: cardinality, decision
making, language, memory, number recognition, number sense, number-word relation,
ordinality, word recognition

To Make:

- On paper, draw 70 circles.

- Print dots in increasing amounts in the first 10 paper circles: one dot in the first circle, two dots in the second circle, three dots in the third circle, and so on until there are 10 dots in the tenth circle. Inside the next 10 circles, write the numerals one through 10 with one number per circle. Next, write the corresponding English word for numbers one through 10 inside the paper circles (one English word per circle). Repeat using the corresponding Spanish word for numbers one (uno) through 10 (diez) inside the paper circles (one Spanish word per circle).

- Carefully cut out each of the 40 paper circles.

- Take the 40 cutout circles—10 with dots, 10 with numerals, 10 with corresponding English words, and 10 with matching Spanish words—and glue one paper circle inside each of the 40 plastic caps of the <u>same</u> color. Set aside to dry. When the glue is dry, store the caps in the bag.

- Return to the sheet of paper with circles drawn on it.
  - Write the numerals one through 10 inside the paper circles (one number per circle). Carefully cut out each of the 10 paper circles.
  - Using 10 plastic caps, which are a <u>different</u> color from the previous 40, glue one paper circle inside each cap. Set aside to dry. When the glue is dry, store the caps in the bag.

- Once again, return to the sheet of paper with circles drawn on it.
  - Write the English word for the numbers one through 10 (one English word per circle). Carefully cut out each of the 10 paper circles.
  - Using 10 plastic caps which are a <u>different</u> color from the previous two sets of plastic caps, glue one paper circle inside each cap. Set aside to dry. When the glue is dry, store the caps in the bag.

- For the last time, return to the sheet of paper with circles drawn on it.
  - Write the Spanish word for the numbers one (uno) through 10 (diez) (one Spanish word per circle). Carefully cut out each of the 10 paper circles.
  - Using 10 plastic caps, which are a <u>different</u> color from the previous three sets of plastic caps, glue one paper circle inside each cap. Set aside to dry. When the glue is dry, store the caps in the bag.

To Play:

On signal, the player empties his or her bag and (1) arranges the caps in numerical order using dots, (2) matches the numeral with the correct number of dots, (3) matches the English word with the numeral, and (4) matches the Spanish word with its numeral and corresponding English word.

- -

Suggestion:

For novices, use the four different colored caps: 10 dot caps of one color; 10 number caps of a different color; 10 English word caps of a third color, and 10 Spanish word caps of a fourth color. As the learner progresses, use only the same colored caps.

Variation:

1. Use languages other than English and Spanish.

VERSION 2:
Sorting Parts of Speech

Making It's in the Bag: Sorting Parts of Speech incorporates and utilizes: dexterity, hand-eye coordination, measurement, parts of speech, writing

Playing It's in the Bag: Sorting Parts of Speech utilizes: data skills (creating and sorting categories), decision making, memory, parts of speech, word recognition

The object of the game is to (1) identify the different parts of speech and (2) group them according to their category.

To Make:

- On paper, draw 30 circles.

- Select 10 words from one part of speech (verbs, for example) and 10 words from a different part of speech (adjectives, for example). Start by writing the 10 verbs inside the paper circles—one verb per circle. Next, write the 10 adjectives inside the paper circles—one adjective per circle.

- Carefully cut out each of the circles.

- Using 20 caps of the same color, glue one paper circle inside each cap. Set aside to dry. When the glue is dry, store the caps in the bag.

Return to the sheet of paper with circles drawn on it.

- Write the same adjectives from the previous step. Carefully cut out each of the paper circles.
- Using 10 plastic caps which are a different color from the previous 20, glue one paper circle inside each cap. Set aside to dry. When the glue is dry, store the caps in the bag.

To Play:

On signal, the players empty their bags and sort by parts of speech.

Suggestion:

For novices, use the two different colored caps: 10 verb caps of one color and 10 adjective caps of the different color. As the learner progresses, use only the same colored caps.

Variations:

1. Use different languages and parts of speech.
2. Act out the words on the caps. Are the actions different depending on the part of speech?

VERSION 3: Shape Sorting

Making It's in the Bag: Shape Sorting incorporates and utilizes: construction of geometric shapes, dexterity, hand-eye coordination

Playing It's in the Bag: Shape Sorting utilizes: data skills (create and sort categories), decision making, geometric shape recognition, memory

To Make:

Cut different-sized circles, diamonds, ovals, parallelograms, rectangles, squares, and triangles from cereal boxes or other tagboard. Shapes should not exceed 4 in by 4 in (10.2 cm x 10.2 cm). Have at least four different sizes for each of the geometric shapes. Put the shapes into a paper bag or drawstring bag.

To Play:

On signal, the players empty his or her bag and sort by shape.

VERSION 4:
Make a Picture of _____

Making It's in the Bag: Make a Picture of _____ incorporates and utilizes:
construction of geometric shapes, dexterity, hand-eye coordination

Playing It's in the Bag: Make a Picture of _____ utilizes: concentration, creativity, decision making, part-whole relationships, spatial relationships

To Make:

Cut different-sized circles, diamonds, ovals, parallelograms, rectangles, squares, and triangles from cereal boxes or other tagboard. Shapes should not exceed 4 in by 4 in (10.2 cm x 10.2 cm). Have at least four different sizes for each of the geometric shapes. Put the shapes into a paper bag or drawstring bag.

To Play:

Players are given the name of an item (e.g., dog, house, tree). On signal, each player empties his or her bag and uses the various shapes to make a representation of that item. This activity is similar to tangrams, but instead of reproducing the silhouette of the tangram puzzle, the task is to create one's own image.

JIANZI

Making Jianzi incorporates and utilizes: dexterity, following directions, hand-eye coordination, problem solving

Playing Jianzi utilizes: balance and flexibility, body-eye coordination, collaboration (when playing with others), concentration, counting, cultural exploration, gross motor skills, movement control, persistence

Jianzi (pronounced schi-an tshe) is a Chinese game that uses a **shuttlecock.** A traditional jianzi is made by wrapping paper around a coin with a hole in the center and then decorating it with feathers (Culin, 1960).

Supplies:

- Ring from the plastic cap on a plastic jug or water bottle
- Plastic grocery bag
- Scissors
- Pencil
- Large eraser

To Make:

- Lay the plastic grocery bag flat on the table. Using scissors, remove the handles and the bottom seam. Smooth out the bag so that it is flat on the surface. Cut the right side from bottom to top, and cut the left side from bottom to top, creating two layers of rectangular plastic. It is OK if the edges are rough.

- With layers together, turn the plastic so the longer side extends out in front.

- Place the plastic ring at the top and center of the plastic sheets.

- With the ring inside, fold the plastic over and over until all the plastic is wrapped around the ring.

- With your fingers, locate the center of the plastic ring. Using the tips of the scissors, cut a small opening through all the layers of sheeting. If this doesn't work, an adult can use the point of the scissors or sharp pencil to poke a small opening through all the layers. Note: When poking through the layers using a pencil, place a large eraser on the table, lay the sheeting over the eraser, and poke down into the eraser.

- Take one end of the folded sheeting and push it through the opening. (A pencil may be helpful in completing this task.) Once through, pull tight.

- Take the other end of the folded sheeting and push it through the opening. Once through, pull tight.

- Using scissors, cut along the folded edges to create a feathered look.

To Play:

- The objective is to keep the jianzi in the air as long as possible using only one's feet and knees.

Suggestions:

- Time how long the jianzi is played without touching the ground.

- Count how many times the jianzi is kicked or tapped with the knee.

- Use different parts of the body (e.g., head, left elbow, back of right hand, shoulder). Count how many different body parts (e.g., left elbow, right elbow, left knee, right knee, head) are used to keep the jianzi in the air.

Variations:

1. Tissue paper; balloons; and shiny, foil-like plastic can replace plastic shopping bags.

2. Use large plastic lids or shoebox lids as paddles to bat the jianzi back and forth between players. Count how many times the jianzi is batted between two players.

3. Form a circle of players and, using only feet or knees, pass the jianzi from one to another. Try to get the jianzi around the entire circle without it touching the ground.

JIANZI

ORDER UP!

Making Order Up! incorporates and utilizes: categorization, creativity, fine motor skills

Playing Order Up! utilizes: decision making, memory, order, sequencing

Supplies:

- Opaque container lids—uniform in size—and at least four per player
- Magazines
- Scissors
- Tape

To Make:

- Cut out images of hats, shirts, pants, and shoes. (Note: Four articles of clothing are needed for an "outfit." Depending on the number of players, include one hat, shirt, pair of pants, and pair of shoes per player.)

- Tape one image to one side of each container lid.

To Play:

- Among the players, decide on the sequence of getting dressed, either starting from the head (hat) or feet (shoes).

- Arrange the lids on a table in a grid with the image side down, and take turns choosing a lid.

- The objective of the game is to get dressed in the correct order. If a player turns over an article of clothing that is not next in the sequence, he or she leaves that piece on the board, flips it back over, and must remember where it is for next time.

Suggestions:

- This game is great for working with children who need to establish a new routine. Therefore, it can be tailored for many situations and transitions. For example, detail all the steps needed to get ready for school in the morning (get out of bed, comb hair, brush teeth, get dressed, eat breakfast, etc.) or to transition to a new activity during the school day (put toys away, walk to a new activity, etc.).

- Bring Order Up! into the math classroom by using it to learn order of operations.

- Try Order Up! for the steps of the scientific method, order of presidents, and chronology of wars or historical time periods as a way to help students remember what or who came first.

- Students can draw representations rather than find images, write text on the lids to describe each step, or include both words and pictures.

PLAY MONEY

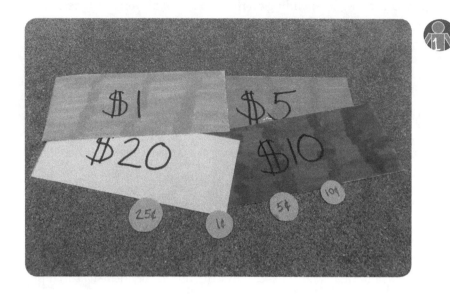

Making Play Money incorporates and utilizes: creativity, dexterity, fine motor skills, geometry (e.g., shape knowledge, spatial relations), measurement, number sense

Playing with Play Money utilizes: arithmetic knowledge, categorization, economics (e.g., currency, **exchange**), number sense, part-whole relationship, sequencing

Supplies:

- Tagboard (cereal boxes, packaging, packing boxes, etc.)
- Card stock (old greeting cards, magazine mailers, junk mail, etc.)
- Pencil
- Scissors
- Dark-colored markers

To Make:

- Decide what denominations of money will be needed. (For example, Will there be pennies only? Coins only? Paper money only?)

- Using the approximate diameters below, draw and cut out coin money from tagboard, OR trace existing coins with a pencil and then cut out.
  - ▲ Penny: 0.75 in (1.9 cm)
  - ▲ Nickel: 0.8 in (2 cm)
  - ▲ Dime: 0.7 in (1.8 cm)
  - ▲ Quarter: 1 in (2.5 cm)
  - ▲ Half Dollar: 1.2 in (3 cm)
  - ▲ Dollar Coin: 1 in (2.5 cm)

- Using the approximate dimensions below, draw and cut out paper money from card stock, OR trace around existing bills with a pencil and then cut out.
  - ▲ Note: U.S. paper money is uniform in size.
  - ▲ Length: 6 in (15.2 cm); width: 2.5 in (6.4 cm)

- Because all bills are the same size, consider making each denomination a different color. Once money is cut out, use a dark-colored marker to write the denomination on the coins and bills. Make sure it is dark enough for everyone to see easily over any pre-existing writing.

To Play:

- Use with My Mini Market (page 64) to make purchases.

- Use with Oink, Oink, Cha-Ching! Piggy Banks (page 22) instead of real money.

Variations:

1. Not all the money in the world is in U.S. denominations. Not all play money needs to be either. What other types of currency do players know about? What other types are there? Is currency always coins and bills? How does bartering work in a similar way to exchanging money for services and goods? Talk about the **exchange rate** and why "one dollar" means something different in different countries.

2. Currency creation: Just as different countries have different forms of currency, so could different classrooms or households. Create your own currency. How will it look? How will it be composed? Will all paper money be uniform in size, as U.S. bills are? How much is each coin and each bill worth, and for what kinds of things could this currency be exchanged in your environment?

ROCK-N-ROLL MATH

Making Rock-n-Roll Math incorporates and utilizes: collaboration on rule making, decision making, measurement

Playing Rock-n-Roll Math utilizes: algebraic skills, algebraic thinking, decision making, problem solving, strategy development, turn taking

Supplies:

- Tagboard, 4 in x 8 in (10.2 cm x 20.3 cm)
- 12 pebbles
- Pair of dice
- Marker
- Straightedge or ruler

To Make:

- Divide and mark the tagboard into 12 squares.
- Number the squares 1 through 12.

To Play:

- The object of the game is to get a pebble in each of the 12 boxes. To begin, roll the dice.
- Decide where pebbles should be placed. There are three choices:
  - ▲ Combine the numbers on the dice and put a pebble on the sum.
  - ▲ Subtract the lower die from the higher die and put a pebble on that number.
  - ▲ Cover the two numbers that correspond with each die.

Suggestions:

- Establish a rule for when game play ends. Also think about the following situations, and establish a rule to follow for when that situation arises.

  - ▲ Can't place a pebble: There will be times when a pebble cannot be placed. Does that mean the game is over? Or is this similar to baseball in which each player gets three strikes? If there are two or more players, should this result in that person losing the game?

  - ▲ Doubles: What happens when a double (same number on each die) is rolled? Does that person get an extra roll? Or does it mean the player loses a turn?

- Incorporate multiplication skills by making a larger board and giving players the option of multiplying numbers together.

Note: This game was named by participants of Big Brothers Big Sisters of Southern Kane and Kendall Counties in Illinois.

SHAPE TOSS

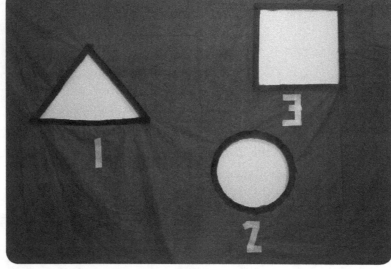

Making Shape Toss incorporates and utilizes: fine motor skills, geometry (knowledge of shapes, Euclidean properties), measurement, planning

Playing Shape Toss utilizes: balance, coordination, gross motor skills, healthy competition skills, identification and labeling of shapes, strategy development, summation, turn taking

Supplies:

- Tarp or old bedsheet
- Colored duct tape
- Markers
- Scissors
- Ruler
- Rope
- Beanbags or other balls, such as a sock filled with birdseed

To Make:

Target

- Find an old tarp or bed sheet. Using a ruler and marker, draw different shapes of varying sizes on the sheet or tarp. For example, draw 10-in (25.4-cm), 12-in (30.5-cm), and 15-in (38.1-cm) squares, diamonds, and/or circles surrounding an 18-in (45.7-cm) center square. These are targets.

- Cut the shapes out of the tarp.

- In the top two corners of the tarp, cut out a hole large enough for the rope to go through. This will be used to hang up the tarp.

- Tape the remaining edges of each cutout with colored duct tape to prevent fraying.

- Using rope, hang the target to a stable structure (fence, two trees, swing set).

Beanbags

- If beanbags or balls are available, use them for this activity. If not, beanbags are very easy to make.
  - ▴ Use old, clean socks (preferably ones without holes in the toes), fill with cloth scraps or birdseed, and tie off the top.

- Do NOT use sand or rocks, as sand easily passes through the sock and rocks create dangerous and heavy bags.
  - ▴ For an even lighter bag, use crumpled-up newspaper, wrapping paper, tissue paper, or socks rolled into a ball.

To Play:

- To practice their passing, aspiring quarterbacks or pitchers can take turns throwing beanbags or balls through the holes from an agreed-upon distance.

- To play this game with younger children, encourage them to identify the shape through which they are tossing the beanbag/ball.

- For older children, use the marker to write a point value (5, 10, and 25; or 1, 2, and 3 for younger children) below each shape target. Use higher values for smaller holes. Encourage each child to keep track of his or her score (i.e., the sum of targets hit) while playing.

SHAPE TOSS

SIMILARITIES

Playing Similarities utilizes: abstract thinking, animal and people knowledge, categorization, color knowledge, communication skills, concentration, decision making, math (e.g., number sense), problem solving, selective attention, spatial relations (e.g., size of objects), vocabulary

Supplies:

- At least 24 fronts of various greeting cards and/or postcards that have pictures or artwork

To Play:

- Place greeting cards facedown in a pile.

- Select any three cards.

- Carefully study them. Identify one common characteristic among all three. For example, all three could have the color red, an animal, a flower, or a summer scene.

- Once the similarity is identified, place the cards back in the pile, shuffle them, and select another three.

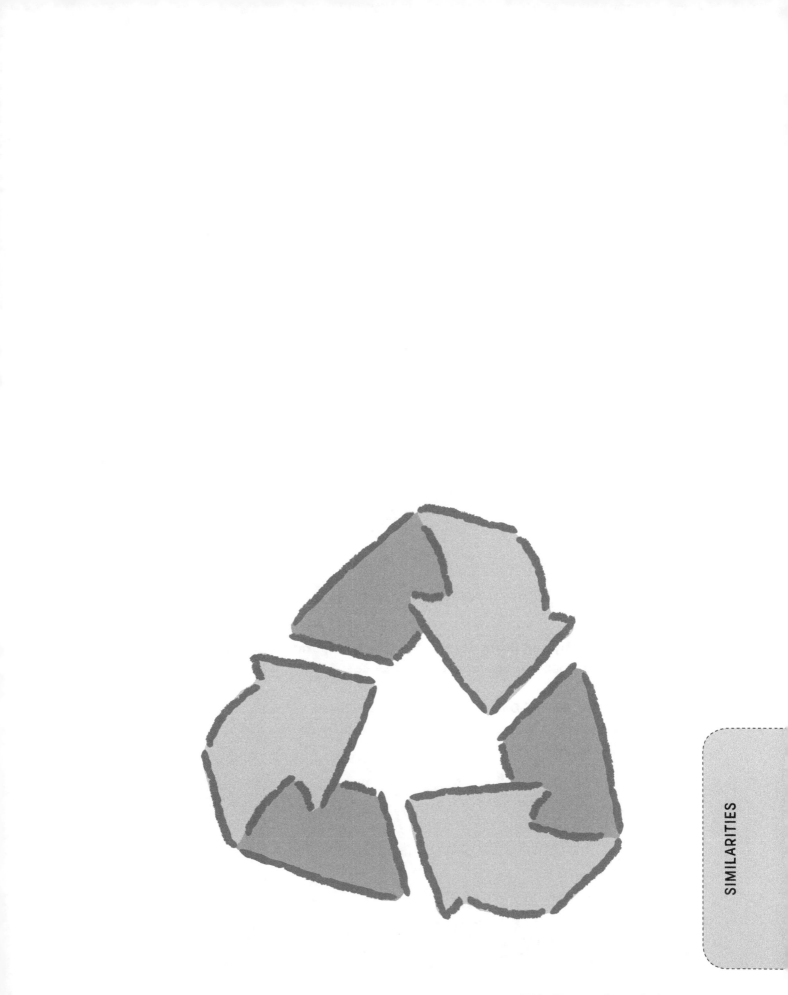

UP AND DOWN
THE NUMBER LINE

Making Up and Down the Number Line incorporates and utilizes: fine motor skills, gross motor skills, measurement, number sense

Playing Up and Down the Number Line utilizes: addition/subtraction, counting, gross motor skills, healthy competition skills, social interaction, turn taking, understanding of number line

Supplies:

- Roll of colorful duct tape or painter's tape, OR package of colored sidewalk chalk
- Large, flat surface
- Yardstick or tape measure
- 2 tin can lids with safely cut, nonsharp edges, OR 2 lids from frozen juice containers
- Permanent marker

To Make:

- If using tape, test on an indiscrete area of the flat surface to make sure the tape will not leave marks when removed. Using tape and the yardstick or tape measure, create a long, skinny rectangle 10 ft (3.7 m) long and 1 ft (30.5 cm) wide. Place a crosspiece of tape at every foot (30.5 cm) so that there are now 10 1-ft x 1-ft (30.5-cm x 30.5-cm) squares in a column. Once the squares are formed, use tape to place numbers consecutively from 1 to 10 in the center of each square.

- If using chalk, simply draw the number line as instructed above.

- On one tin lid, write the number 1 on both sides with permanent marker. On the other, write the number 2 on both sides.

To Play:

- Once the number line is complete, each player tosses a lid down the line. Similar to hopscotch, players must jump down the line, counting as they go, until they reach their target number.

- When they retrieve their lid, they must jump back, also counting.

- Each child must keep track of his or her target numbers, adding them together from turn to turn. This is the player's score.

- At the end of five rounds, the child with the highest score wins. Or perhaps it is the lowest score. Each game may have a slightly different way to win.

Suggestions:

- For older children, bring multiplication skills in by requiring them to count by multiples of 2, 3, 4, etc.

- Bring in further competition by requiring the winning score to be a particular number or a particular kind of number (e.g., multiple of 7, prime number, perfect square, etc.).

- Promote cooperation by having one person jump to his or her square and the second person jump to his or her square. As a team, they must then agree on either the sum or product of the two numbers.

CHAPTER 6
Spinning, Rolling, Floating

A family sits in the living room, playing a word game in which the objective is to get others to say a target word or phrase without using the common descriptors.

Mother: *Sometimes you see these annoying things when you're motoring on the avenues.*

Father: *Drivers?*

Mother: *No, it's more a part of the avenues themselves.*

Father: *Speed limits?*

Mother: *No, no. Oh! You might get a flat tire if you go over one.*

Child: *A cliff!*

It is fair to say that the child in this story has a rudimentary understanding of the effects of motion as well as a slick sense of humor, but he might benefit from a little more interaction with games that explore movement and objects in motion. The activities in this chapter will do just that. Check out the effects of wind while constructing and playing with kites and pinwheels, or learn about potential and kinetic energy with whizzers. And remember, a body in play stays in play!

(Psst: The answer was a pothole.)

Games in This Chapter:

- **Buoyancy or Bust:** Construct a paper boat that can withstand more weight than competitors' boats.

- **Kite:** Investigate properties of flight by designing a kite.

- **Mini Spinnies:** Spin and battle tiny tops.

- **Pint-Sized Parachute:** Explore concepts of objects in motion and gravity by creating parachutes that are easy to tuck away in a pencil box or pocket.

- **Pinwheel:** Design a wind-powered toy.

- **Rain Stick:** Think about the relationship between sound and motion with this soothing instrument.

- **Toothpaste Box Glider:** Experiment with balance to achieve lift and distance.

- **Tubes of Fun:** Apply principles of geometry to create a path for a ball using cardboard tubes.

- **Twirlybird:** Test the effects different sizes and weights of paper on rotational motion and air resistance.

- **T'wis:** Play a game of skill played by the Woodland Indians.

- **'Ulu Maika:** Compete in a game of skill played by early Hawaiians.

- **Whizzer:** Create a simple handheld game to learn about sound and airflow.

BUOYANCY OR BUST

Making Buoyancy or Bust incorporates and utilizes: creativity, dexterity, measurement, planning, problem-solving skills, understanding of buoyancy

Playing Buoyancy or Bust utilizes: healthy competition skills, planning, problem solving, strategy development, understanding of balance/counterbalance, buoyancy, and displacement

Supplies:

- Large tub of water, big enough to hold two competitors' boats at once
- 1–2 sheets of paper (newspaper, magazine pages, other scrap paper) per player
- 100 weights, all the same, such as small plastic caps, paper clips, or marbles—more if needed
- Paper and pencil to record results

To Make:

- The objective of Buoyancy or Bust is to create a boat that will float longer than the competitor's boat when more and more weight is placed inside.

- Each participant must design and build a boat using only the paper provided. Make sure that each player has the same amount of paper to work with. The player may then decide how much of his or her allotted paper to use. Remember, no other materials should be used in constructing the boat (no tape, no glue). The boat must be able to take on weight.

- Remember to name the boats!

- Each player now creates a log sheet with the name of his or her boat on top and a space next to it for the competitor's boat. Leave space below to fill in information about what happens every time one weight is added.

To Play:

- Fill a large tub (shallow storage bins work nicely) with water. Two at a time, participants float their boats in the water. Each participant should be prepared to record information about his or her competition on a sheet of paper.

- The first step is to determine whether each boat floats on its own. If one does not float, it is out of the competition. Another boat and participant should take its place. When two boats float on their own, the second step of the battle can begin.

- Alternating turns, players add one weight at a time to their boats. On their paper, players record the number of weights and the effect on their boat and their competitor's (e.g., no change, leaning left, sank, etc.). Players must decide where and how to introduce each weight to their boat. The individual whose boat stays floating the longest is the winner. If both boats hold up, subsequent rounds may be held and a grand champion determined.

Suggestions:

- Think about or answer the following questions about Buoyancy or Bust, and decide how the answers could be used to create a more effective boat.
  - ▲ What factor(s) ultimately sank the boats?
  - ▲ What design features best kept the boats floating?
  - ▲ What strategies of adding weight worked best to keep the boats floating?

- Play around with altering the rules of the game.
  - ▲ Leave choice of building material up to each student (removing uniformity).
  - ▲ Have players add weights to the <u>competitor's</u> boat.
    - • Note: Players should know this in advance.
  - ▲ Introduce motion by attaching a string to the **bow** of each boat. Players must pull their boat across the tub after each weight is introduced without tipping or sinking the boat.
  - ▲ Alter the fluid:
    - • Stir in 1 cup (240 mL) of salt for each quart (960 mL) of water.
    - • Stir in 1 cup (240 mL) of cornstarch for each quart (960 mL) of water.
    - • Does buoyancy change in a different liquid? Why or why not?

KITE

Making the Kite incorporates and utilizes: attributes of shapes and angles, dexterity, geometry, hand-eye coordination, measurement, science of nature

Playing with the Kite utilizes: fine motor skills, gross motor skills, science of flight (e.g., airflow, gravity, lift)

Supplies:

- Stick, approximately 3 ft (91.4 cm) in length, 0.5 in (1.3 cm) in diameter
- Stick, approximately 2 ft (61 cm) in length, 0.5 in (1.3 cm) in diameter
- 1–2 full sheets of newspaper (enough to cover kite face)
- 500 ft (152 m) of twine or coarse string
- Scissors
- Tape
- Used ribbon (optional)

To Make:

- Begin with a search for sticks. Choose sticks that have fallen to the ground as they have already died. Pulling limbs off of trees is harming a living thing. Set the sticks on a flat surface in the shape of a plus sign. One stick will be on top of the other and wobble. Holding the plus sign stable, begin wrapping the end of the roll of twine around <u>both</u> sticks in a crisscross manner, leaving a 6-in (15.2-cm) "tail" at the start. The sticks should be wrapped well enough that they hold the plus sign shape without help. Tie the end of the twine around the 6-in (15.2-cm) tail, close to the center of the plus sign. Trim the other end of the twine from the roll.

- Beginning at the bottom of the long stick, tie a new piece of twine tightly near the end (farthest from the center of the plus sign). Bring the twine up to the right end of the shorter stick and wrap it around that stick three or four times. Now bring the twine up to the top of the long stick, wrapping it three or four times around its end. Make sure to wrap it tightly. Bring the twine down to the left end of the shorter stick and, again, wrap it tightly around that end three or four times. Finally, bring the twine back down to the bottom of the long stick, and tie it tightly. Trim this twine from the roll.

- Lay the kite frame on top of newspaper. Fold each side of the newspaper up and over each section of twine, and tape the newspaper corners to the inside of the kite, but leave a 6-in (15.2-cm) tail sticking out. There should now be a solid kite face in place.

- Tie the end of the roll of twine to the 6-in (15.2-cm) tail of twine remaining at the center of the kite. Do not trim it as this will be the length of twine for flying.

- Optional: Tie a separate 2- to 3-ft (61- to 91.4-cm) length of string to the 6-in (15.2-cm) tail of twine remaining at the center of the kite. Tie used ribbons around this piece of twine at even intervals. This is the kite's tail.

To Play:

- Choose a windy day. Holding the kite at arm's length in one hand and the end or roll of string in the other, begin running into the wind. As the wind catches the kite, release it.

- Keep running to allow the kite to soar higher into the sky. Once the kite feels stable, stop running and hold onto the string. When the kite falls to the ground, begin again.

- To make the kite return to the ground, slacken the string by walking toward the kite.

KITE

Suggestions:

- What happens if the shape of the kite is different, such as a taller diamond or a square? What about a triangle-shaped kite? Will these fly?

- Instead of newspaper, try a different material to cover the kite: tissue paper, construction paper, fabric, etc. Will the kite still fly? Does it fly differently? Why might the material used make a difference, if it does?

- This science- and math-based activity could be incorporated into a history lesson on Benjamin Franklin or an exploration into the multicultural sport of kite fighting.

MINI SPINNIES

Making Mini Spinnies incorporates and utilizes: following directions, measurement, patience, problem solving

Playing Mini Spinnies utilizes: fine motor skills, patience, problem solving, scientific concepts (e.g., balance, force, mass, motion, rotation)

Supplies:

- Soft plastic cap from plastic jugs
- Round bamboo skewer, 12 in x 0.1 in (30.5 cm x 0.3 cm)
- Eraser or multi-folded hand towel
- Ruler
- Pliers
- Markers, optional

To Make:

- Place the eraser or multi-folded hand towel on a flat surface. Place the plastic cap on top with the open side down. Identify the <u>exact</u> center of the cap. Place the point of the skewer at the <u>exact</u> center of the cap and firmly press down until the skewer pierces the cap and goes into the eraser or cloth.

- Once the skewer is all the way through, measure 6 in (15.2 cm) from the sharp end, and break off the sharp end of the skewer or cut with the wire-cutting section of the pliers.

To Play:

- Start off with the cap at the midpoint of the 6-in (15.2-cm) skewer segment. Test the top by giving it a spin using your thumb and index finger. Note: Weight and design differences exist among caps: Some caps need a longer axis while others need a shorter one.
  - ▲ If the spin is wobbly, adjust the cap up or down until achieving a smooth spin.
  - ▲ If moving the cap up or down doesn't do the trick, shorten the stick by 1 in (2.5 cm).

- Spin again.
  - ▲ What is the longest time the top spun?
  - ▲ Does it spin longer with the cap positioned more toward the top or more toward the bottom of the axis?

Suggestions:

- Create an interesting visual effect by drawing a spiral on the outer flat part of the cap. Start at the center of the cap and gradually circle around to the edge. Spin the top and pay attention to the spiral. Now spin the top in the opposite direction while paying attention to the spiral. What did you see?

- Make a larger top using the soft, plastic lid from a deli container [5–6 inches (12.7–15.2 cm) in diameter].

Variation:

1. Challenge friends to a "spin-off." The top that spins the longest wins.

PINT-SIZED PARACHUTE

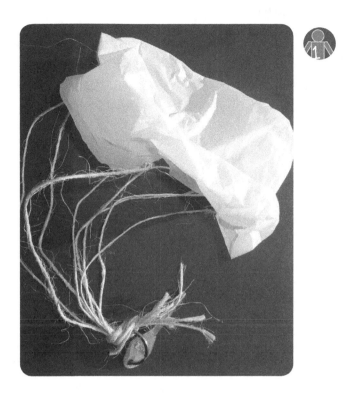

Making the Pint-Sized Parachute incorporates and utilizes: dexterity, fine motor skills, geometry (properties of angles, polygons), measurement

Playing with the Pint-Sized Parachute utilizes: gross motor skills, hand-eye coordination, motion of falling objects, resistance, science of airflow, theory of gravity

Supplies:

- Plastic grocery bag
- Scissors
- Ruler
- Pen
- Hole punch
- Tape
- 8 pieces of string or yarn, each 16 in (40.6 cm) long
- Figurine or weighted item to be the parachutist

To Make:

- Lay the plastic bag flat on a table so that it folds as it originally was folded. Carefully cut off the handles of the bag.

- Using the bottom edge and one of the side edges as guides, mark with the ruler and pen a square that measures 12 in x 12 in (30.5 cm x 30.5 cm). With scissors, cut the square out of one side of the plastic bag. (Individuals may want to team up and use one bag. They can cut both sides together to yield 2 parachute pieces.) Discard the extra pieces of plastic.

- Using the ruler and a pen, make a mark on each side of the square every 3 in (7.6 cm). Each side should then have three marks, one at 3 in (7.6 cm), one at 6 in (15.2 cm), and one at 9 in (22.9 cm).

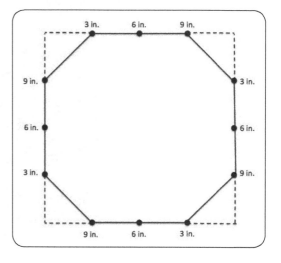

- Starting with the left side, locate the top mark. Cut a straight line from that mark to the 3-in (7.6-cm) mark on the top of the square. This should remove the corner of the square. Turn the plastic square 90 degrees to the left and repeat until all four corners of the square have been removed. Discard the removed corners. What is left is an octagon.

- Place a small piece of tape, about 1 in (2.5 cm) square at every corner of the octagon and on <u>both</u> sides of the plastic. The tape will reinforce the plastic where the string ties on.

- Using the hole punch, make a hole in the center of each piece of tape on the plastic for a total of eight holes (placement does not have to be exactly even at each corner).

- Insert one piece of string into each hole and tie into a knot around the outside of the bag. Tie the loose ends of all the strings securely around the parachutist.

To Play:

Find a high spot, such as on a chair or at the top of the stairs. Drop the parachute and observe its fall.

Suggestions:

- Does the object at the end of the parachute fall the same way when it is not attached to a parachute?

- Does the weight of the parachutist affect how quickly it falls?

- Does the size of the parachutist affect how quickly it falls?

- What would it take to keep the parachutist in the air without touching it?
  - ▴ Blowing on it?
  - ▴ Flapping a piece of tagboard under it?
  - ▴ Using a hair dryer?

- What would happen if the parachutist was dropped in a vacuum?
  - ▴ Warning: Be sure kids know we are talking about space without air, not the household appliance. We do not want to get any vacuum cleaner repair bills!

PINWHEEL

Making the Pinwheel incorporates and utilizes: dexterity, following directions, hand-eye coordination, measurement

Playing with the Pinwheel utilizes: creativity, decision making, exploration of the scientific method, problem solving, science of airflow, simple machines (e.g., axle, wheel)

Supplies:

- Cereal box or any thick, sturdy piece of paper (newspaper advertisement)
- Markers, crayons, or paint
- Pen
- Scissors
- Ruler
- Pushpin
- Pencil with a good eraser
- Multi-folded hand towel
- Tape
- Aluminum foil, glue, optional

To Make:

- Measure and cut a square out of the sturdy paper.

- Using the ruler, create four **quadrants** by measuring and marking the midpoint of each side of the paper square and connecting them with lines.

- Decorate each area using markers, crayons, or paint.
  - ▲ Fill in each area with a different color.
  - ▲ Glue on aluminum foil, which will reflect the light.
  - ▲ Note: If using paint or glue, wait for it to dry before moving to the next step.

- Place your finger at the very center of the paper square and trace around it.

- Make four diagonal lines starting from each outside corner of the paper and stopping at the outline of your fingertip.

- Cut each diagonal line to create a triangular shape. Do NOT cut beyond the fingertip line.

- Fold alternating points into the center and tape to hold them in place.

- Place the paper pinwheel on top of the multi-folded towel. At the center point, insert the pushpin through the overlapping pieces.

- Remove the paper pinwheel from the towel and place the pencil on top of the towel. Align the point of the pin with the eraser on the pencil. Press.
  - ▲ Note: Make sure there is room between the pushpin and the pinwheel or it will not spin correctly.

To Play:

- Introduce the pinwheel to airflow (blow on it, place it in front of a fan, take it outside on a windy day), and observe its motion. Answer the following questions to explore the scientific method (ask questions, make predictions, set up tests, find the answers):
  - ▲ Does the speed of the spinning change depending on the direction the pinwheel is held?
  - ▲ Does the speed of the spinning change depending on the strength of the airflow?
  - ▲ Can the shape of the wheel's blades be changed to affect the spinning?

Suggestion:

- Experiment with paper size to make larger and smaller pinwheels. Does the size of the pinwheel change the rate of spin?

RAIN STICK

Making the Rain Stick incorporates and utilizes: decision making, dexterity, estimation, trial-and-error skills

Playing with the Rain Stick utilizes: creativity, cultural exploration, listening, perspective-taking skill (thinking of other cultures), trial and error, understanding properties of motion
and sound

Supplies:

- Paper towel tube
- 4 pieces of wax paper, 5 in (12.7 cm) square
- 4 rubber bands
- 8 toothpicks
- 16 .5-in (1.3-cm) square pieces of duct, masking, or painter's tape
- Crayons, colored pencils, or markers
- ½ cup of small pebbles
- Scissors

To Make:

- Wrap one open end of the paper towel tube tightly with two squares of wax paper and secure with a rubber band. Fold the excess wax paper back over the rubber band toward the end of the tube and secure it with a second rubber band.

- Carefully insert the toothpicks through the paper towel tube—from one side to the other—making sure to leave enough room at the other end to seal it with wax paper. Push each toothpick through the whole diameter of the tube at different angles to create varied movement of pebbles inside. Trim any sharp ends that extend outside of the tube with scissors, and cover each trimmed end with a tape square. The rain stick can now be decorated, if desired.

- Carefully drop pebbles into the tube, listening to the sound they make as they fall. If more or varied sound is desired, add more toothpicks. With all the pebbles inside the tube, secure the open end with the remaining two squares of wax paper and two rubber bands.

To Play:

- Turn the tube slowly so that pebbles fall from one covered end to the other.

- Listen to the sound the pebbles make as they fall. Also listen to the sound when the tube is turned more quickly, turned at a different angle, or rolled across a surface.

Suggestions:

- Use this activity in a lesson about the properties of sound:
  - ▲ How do different-sized pebbles change the sound and why?
  - ▲ Why might the pebbles hitting different-sized sticks make a different sound?

- Use this activity when talking about cultures that incorporate rain sticks and other similar intervening instruments:
  - ▲ Does your culture include them?
  - ▲ Why are they used and what do they do?
  - ▲ How were they used in history and do these uses differ from those of today?

- If your culture does not use such instruments, are there any similar items in use? How are they similar? How are they different?

Variation:

1. Instead of pebbles, use different fillers, such as can tabs, wooden beads, or other small items. Does the sound change? What does it sound like? This may no longer be a rain stick. What might it be called?

TOOTHPASTE BOX GLIDER

Making the Toothpaste Box Glider incorporates and utilizes: calculation, dexterity, following directions, geometry, hand-eye coordination, measurement, patience

Playing with the Toothpaste Box Glider utilizes: balance, fine motor skills, gross motor skills, measurement, patience, persistence, science of flight, symmetry, trial-and-error learning

Supplies:

- Packaging box for toothpaste (approximately 9 in x 2 in x 1.5 in) (22.9 cm x 5.1 cm x 3.8 cm)
- 2 or 3 pennies
- 1 or 2 jumbo paper clips
- Tape
- Scissors
- Ruler
- Utility or craft knife

To Make:

- Cut along each of the lengthwise edges of the box to make four rectangles: two that are approximately 11.25 in x 2 in (28.6 cm x 5.1 cm), including the tabs, and two that are approximately 11.25 in x 1.5 in (28.6 cm x 3.8 cm), including the tabs. The wider rectangles will become the body of the glider and the wing; the skinnier rectangles will be used for the horizontal stabilizer at the tail of the glider.

Form the body of the glider.

- Take one of the 11.25-in x 2-in (28.6-cm x 5.1-cm) rectangles. Remove the tabs. Fold it in half lengthwise to form a 9-in x 1-in (22.9-cm x 2.5-cm) rectangle and seal both ends with tape.

- Two slits will be cut lengthwise along the <u>midline</u> and through both layers of the folded tagboard. Select one end to be the nose of the glider. From the tip of the nose, measure 1.25 in (3.2 cm) and make a mark. From that mark, measure 3.25 in (8.3 cm) and make another mark. Draw a line between these two marks. Along the line, cut through both layers. (This slit will be for the wing.)

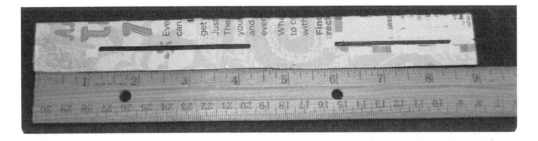

- Starting again from the nose of the glider, measure 6.25 in (15.9 cm) and make a mark. From that mark, measure 2.25 in (5.7 cm). Draw a line between these two marks. Along the line, cut through both layers. (This slit will be for the horizontal stabilizer.) Set aside.

Make the wing.

- The wing is made from the 11.25-in x 2-in (28.6-cm x 5.1-cm) rectangle. The tabs are part of the wing; <u>do not remove the tabs</u>. Starting at either end, measure 5.1 in (13 cm), and draw a line across the width. This is the centerline.

- Next, calculate 45 percent of the distance from the centerline to each wing tip; mark the distance and draw a line across the width of the wing. There are two 45-percent lines—one to the left of the centerline and one to the right of the centerline

- Find the midpoint on each 45-percent line. Using a ruler or straightedge, draw a line connecting these midpoints and extending out to each wing tip. This is the midline.

- At the tips, measure and mark 0.25 in (0.6 cm) on each side of the midline. Using a ruler or straightedge, draw lines connecting the 45-percent line to the .25-in (0.6-cm) marks at the wing tips. Cut along these diagonal lines.

- Fold the wing in half with wing tips touching, and gently crease. Set aside.

Make the horizontal stabilizer that goes in the tail section.

- Take one of the 11.25-in x 1.5-in (28.6-cm x 3.8-cm) rectangle pieces and remove the tabs. Measure and cut a 5-in (12.7-cm) length.

- Calculate the midpoint of the length, and draw a line. From each tip of the stabilizer, measure 1 in (2.5 cm), and draw a line. Make a fold at each 1-in (2.5-cm) line.

Assemble.

- Insert the wing through the large [3.25-in (8.3-cm)] slit in the body of the glider. The centerline of the wing must be in alignment with the body. At the centerline fold, make a slight upward bend of the wing. Do the same with both tip folds.

- Insert the horizontal stabilizer through the smaller slit. The centerline of the stabilizer needs to be in alignment with the body. Make slight upward bends in the folds at the tips.

To Play:

This is where the fun in problem solving starts. Have the pennies, paper clips, scissors, and tape handy while working out the balance of the aircraft. Test the glider in an open area, taking care not to throw it directly toward another person. Make sure the throwing hand is kept parallel to the ground when releasing the glider.

- Up-down dives
  - If, after the release, the glider takes a <u>sudden</u> sharp angle up <u>toward the sun</u>, the nose is too light. Make a small cut in the tape at the nose of the plane, insert one penny, and reseal with tape. Test again. Add pennies as needed. Given this design, no more than three pennies should be needed.
  - If, after the release, the glider takes a <u>sudden</u> sharp dive <u>toward the ground</u>, the nose is too heavy. Make a small cut in the tape at the tail of the plane, insert one penny, and reseal with tape. Test again. Add pennies as needed.

- Left-right dives
  - If, after the release, the glider takes a sharp turn to the <u>left</u>, the glider is heavier on the left side. Add a paper clip to the right wing somewhere before the first bend. Experiment to find the best spot. Test again. If changing the location of the paper clip does not affect the flight path, add another paper clip.

▲ If, after the release, the glider takes a sharp turn to the <u>right</u>, the glider is heavier on the right side. Add a paper clip to the left wing somewhere before the first bend. Experiment to find the best spot. Test again. If changing the location of the paper clip does not affect the flight path, add another paper clip.

▲ For more subtle adjustments, move the wing forward or back in the slit. In addition, make slight increases or decreases to the angle of the bends in the wing and/or the horizontal stabilizer.

Suggestions:

- Measure the distance the glider travels. What is the longest?
  ▲ Throw the glider 10 times. Graph the distances. Calculate the average distance.

- Measure the amount of time the glider stays in the air.
  ▲ Throw the glider 10 times. Graph the times. Calculate the average time in the air.

- Be mindful of your body position as you launch the glider. How do you affect the distance achieved? How do you affect the amount of time the glider stays in the air?

- The design of this glider was created and tested by one of the author's sons who studies aerospace engineering and does research at the National Institute for Aviation Research. But this isn't the only glider design there is. Now that you know some of the basic mechanics of flight, create your own design.

Variation:

1. Organize a competition to see whose glider can go the farthest and whose glider can stay in the air the longest.

   a. Is the glider that goes the farthest the same glider that stays in the air the longest?

TOOTHPASTE BOX GLIDER

TUBES OF FUN

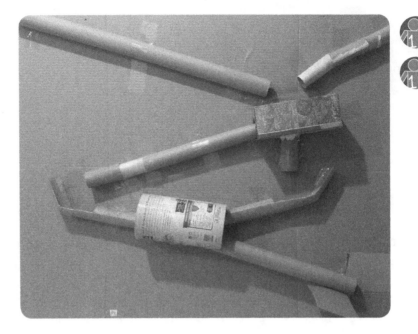

Making Tubes of Fun incorporates and utilizes: angles, creativity, decision making, experimentation, geometry, fine motor skills, measurement, trial and error

Playing Tubes of Fun utilizes: cooperation, decision making, geometry, prediction

Supplies:

- 48-in x 36-in (121.9-cm x 91.4-cm) piece of cardboard
- At least 10 paper tubes of varying lengths
  - ▲ 4–6 in (10.2–15.2 cm)
  - ▲ 30 in (76.2 cm)
- 15-cup (1,260-mL) oatmeal container
- Tissue box
- Aluminum foil crumbled into several balls
- Packing or duct tape
- Scissors

To Make:

The objective of Tubes of Fun is to use the most tubes and create the longest or most creative path for the balls to roll through, starting at the top of the board.

- Set the display board or piece of cardboard next to a wall or two chairs and secure with tape if needed.

- Use scissors to cut long tubes into a variety of lengths.

- Cut holes in the tissue box and oatmeal container to join tubes and create connections.

- Experiment with the placement of the tubes on the board by placing them at various angles. Secure them to the board with tape.

- Connect tubes so that balls fall or roll from one tube into the next.

To Play:

- Place the ball at the top of the board and let it roll through the tube paths.

Suggestions:

- What happens to the ball if the tube is angled differently?

- What makes the ball speed up or slow down?

- Does the diameter of the tube affect speed?

- Guess how long it will take for the ball to race to the bottom. Which path will take the least time? Why? Test your hypothesis.

- Measure the angles of the tubes. Is there a relationship between how quickly the ball completes the course and the angles of the tubes?

Variations:

1. Take turns with a partner so that each person has a chance to arrange a tube on the board.

2. Create multiple paths to race the balls down the board.

TWIRLYBIRD

Making Twirlybird incorporates and utilizes: following directions, hand-eye coordination, measurement, spatial relations

Playing Twirlybird utilizes: experimentation, problem solving, trial and error

Supplies:

- Different weighted paper (tablet paper, construction paper, tagboard, wax paper, aluminum foil)
- Ruler
- Scissors
- Paper clips, optional

To Make:

- Cut a piece of paper into the shape of a rectangle.

- Set the rectangle on a flat surface so that the longest sides are vertical and the shortest sides are horizontal.

- Number the sides 1, 2, 3, and 4 clockwise, starting from the top.

- At side 1, cut a long slit toward the center of the paper, but stop short of the center.

- On side 2, cut a short slit toward the center, again stopping short of the midpoint. Do the same on side 4.

- Fold the bottom half of sides 4 and 2 into the center so the flaps overlap.

- Gently fold the "blades" from side 1 in opposite directions so they look like the letter "T."

- Create a "V," or hook, at the bottom by folding the paper.

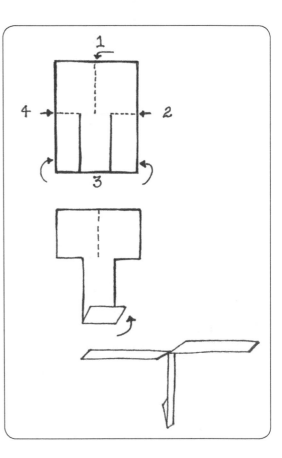

To Play:

- Toss Twirlybird in the air.

- Pay attention to how Twirlybird spins.

Suggestions:

- Try making different-sized rectangles to cut and fold into Twirlybirds. Do smaller Twirlybirds spin faster?

- Try different types/weights of paper. Does the weight of the material affect the rate of spinning?

- Add a paper clip to the tip. What happens when weight is attached?

TWIRLYBIRD

T'WIS

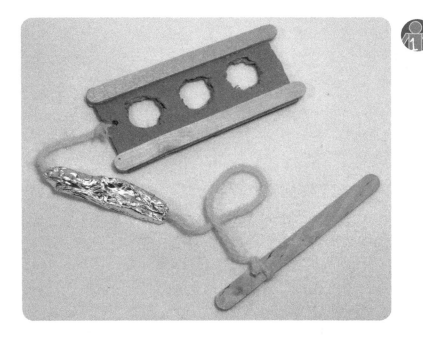

Making T'wis incorporates and utilizes: fine motor skills, hand-eye coordination, measurement, planning

Playing T'wis utilizes: coordination, cultural exploration, hand-eye coordination, patience, persistence, probability, summation

T'wis is one type of a bundle-and-pin game of skill created and played by North American Indians. Original versions are composed of animal hide, twigs, bone, and/or sinew. While there are regional differences in design, the objective of the game is the same: to flip an attached target into the air and catch it on the end of a sharp stick or bone (Prindle, 2013).

Supplies:

- Cardboard, 2 in x 4 in (5.1 cm x 10.2 cm), OR a 2-in x 8-in (5.1-cm x 20.3-cm) piece of tagboard folded in half to create a 2-in x 4-in (5.1-cm x 10.2-cm) rectangle (glue the inner sides together)
- 5 craft sticks [0.4 in x 4.25 in(1 cm x 10.8 cm)]
- String [14 in (35.6 cm)]
- Strip of aluminum foil, 4 in x 2 in (10.2 cm x 5.1 cm)
- Glue   >*Supplies continued*

- Pencil
- Eraser or multi-folded hand towel
- Penny
- Scissors

To Make:

- Mark and cut three penny-sized holes vertically on the cardboard so that it resembles a traffic light.

- Lengthwise, along each side of the holes and on both sides of the cardboard, glue a craft stick and let dry.

- With the tip of a sharpened pencil, rest the cardboard on top of an eraser or folded hand towel on a flat surface and poke a fourth hole below the three holes. Use this hole to attach one end of the string.

- Thread the string through this fourth hole and tie to secure. Tie the other end of the string around the middle of a craft stick, and trim the excess string.

- Fold the aluminum foil in half to create a 2-in (5.1-cm) strip. Roughly 2 in (5.1 cm) from where the string is attached to the cardboard, wrap the string with the narrow width of the foil, creating a 2-in- (5.1-cm-) wide bundle or weight.

- Note: The purpose of the foil bundle is to aid in the maneuvering of the cardboard. Move it closer and/or farther from the cardboard to find the best spot for it on the string.

To Play:

- Hold the stick with your thumb and index finger.

- Using your wrist, flip the cardboard into the air, and catch it by poking the stick through one of the holes.

Suggestions:

- Assign points to the three holes.
  - ▴ See how many points you can get in five catches. What would be the maximum number of points possible? What would be the least number of points possible?
  - ▴ Try to get as many points possible with the least number of catches.

Variation:

1. Compete with others. The first person to reach 10 points wins.

ʻULU MAIKA

Making ʻUlu Maika incorporates and utilizes: cultural exploration, cultural symbolism, fine motor skills, measurement, personal expression

Playing ʻUlu Maika utilizes: balance, coordination, focused attention, gross motor skills, healthy competition skills, movement control, problem solving, social interaction, spatial relations, strategy development, summation, turn taking, understanding of objectives and rules

ʻUlu maika (pronounced *oo-loo ma-ee-ka*) is a game that was played by early Hawaiians. The aim of the game is to roll a disc between two narrowly placed goals a distance away. A 500-ft (152.4-m) ʻulu maika playing field can be found on the island of Molokaʻi (Hawaiian Games, 2010).

Supplies:

- 3 plastic bottles filled with water
- Empty tape roll or empty ribbon spool for each player
- Markers

To Make:

Using markers, decorate the empty tape roll. A player can make up a design or research and incorporate historical and cultural ones.

To Play:

- Agree on the distance between the goal and the point where the discs are released.

- At the goal, place two bottles. The space between the bottles should be approximately 4–6 in (10.2–15.2 cm) wider than the width of the disc being rolled.

- From the goal, measure the agreed-upon distance and place the third bottle to designate the release line.

- Players take turns rolling their disc. To score a point, the disc must roll between the two bottles. The first person to get his or her disc through the goal five times wins.

  ▲ Note: The rolling distance can increase as skill level increases. The space between the bottles can also vary depending on skill level, starting wider with a novice and narrowing as aim improves.

Suggestions:

- Use different-sized discs and assign a different point value for each size.

- Create a ramp using a cardboard box. Instead of hand-rolling the disc, use the ramp to launch the disc.
  ▲ Does the angle of the ramp make a difference?

- Form and compete as teams.

'ULU MAIKA

WHIZZER

Making the Whizzer incorporates and utilizes: dexterity, hand-eye coordination, measurement

Playing with the Whizzer utilizes: coordination, kinetic energy, potential energy, transfer of energy

Supplies:

- 2 paper plates
- Pencil, sharpened
- Old shoelace or 2-ft (61-cm) length of string, ribbon, or yarn (not nylon)
- Crayons, colored pencils, or markers
- Tape

To Make:

- Place two paper plates face-to-face, so that the lips of the plates are touching each other. This should form a hollow disc. Tape the two plates together at four evenly spaced places around the circumference of the disc.

- Punch two holes all the way through both plates using the sharpened pencil. These two holes should be next to one another, each 1–1.5 in (2.5–3.8 cm) from the center of the plates. Run the pencil all the way through the holes to make them nice and big. The disc should now resemble a large, 2-holed button and have a total of 4 holes—2 in each plate.

- Place the shoelace through one set of holes and then back through the holes next to it. The plates can be pinched together to make stringing easier. Grab both loose ends of the shoelace and hold them up so that the disc falls to the bottom (it might need to be coaxed). Tie the loose ends of the string together.

- Holding the tied ends with one hand, grab the string on the other side of the paper plates with the other hand. It will likely be right up against the face of the disc, so it might have to be pulled a little. The goal is to get the disc to be in the center of the loop.

To Play:

- Place a thumb and forefinger from each hand into each side of the loop of string. Holding one hand still, move the other hand in a circular motion to wind the Whizzer. The string should begin to twist around itself.

- When the string is all twisted up, pull your hands apart and listen for whizzing.

- To reload the Whizzer, bring your hands closer together and pull again.

Suggestions:

- Before stringing the plates onto the laces, decorate the disc on both sides to see what happens to the artwork during spinning.

- Try different lengths of string. Does the spinning change with different lengths of string?

- Before taping the plates together, glue different materials (e.g., yarn, paper, wax paper, old playing cards) to the inside so that they extend beyond the edge of the plates when taped together. These materials should form "arms." Take note of what noise different arms make.
  - ▲ Does a more rigid arm make a different sound than a less rigid arm?
  - ▲ Do various arms make the disc spin differently?

Person-Activity Table
Number of People Needed to Play

CHAPTER	ACTIVITY	GAME PLAY	VARIATIONS
2: GO THE DISTANCE	Give Yourself a Hand	1 person	1. 2 people / 3 people
	Oink, Oink, Cha-Ching! Piggy Banks	1 person	
	Paper Chain Measuring Tape	1 person	
	Recycle Racer	2 people / 3 people	1. 2 people / 3 people
	Reuse Choo-Choo	2 people / 3 people	1. 2 people / 3 people
	Ring Toss	2 people / 3 people	1. 2 people / 3 people
	Skateboard	2 people / 3 people	1. 2 people / 3 people
	Snow Snake	2 people / 3 people	1. 2 people 2. 3 people 3. 3 people
	Zip Line Balloon:	1 person / 2 people	1. 2 people

CHAPTER	ACTIVITY	GAME PLAY	VARIATIONS
3: FORETHOUGHT	Achi	👤1 👤2	
	Ball in a Cup	👤1	1. 👤1
	Bowling	👤1 👤2 👤3 / 👤1 👤2 👤3	1. 👤1 👤2 👤3
	Bring 'em Home	👤1	
	Discus Bull's-Eye	👤1 👤2 / 👤1 👤2 👤3	
	Kick the Wicket	👤1 👤2 👤3	
	Knucklebones	👤1	
	Mancala	👤1 👤2	
	Mini Golf	👤1 👤2 / 👤1 👤2 👤3	
	My Mini Market	👤1 👤2 👤3	
	Peanut Plunge	👤1 👤2	1. 👤1 👤2 2. 👤1 👤2
	Puzzles	👤1	1. 👤1 👤2
	Senses of Touch	👤1 👤2 / 👤1 👤2 👤3	

CHAPTER	ACTIVITY	GAME PLAY	VARIATIONS
4: AMALGAMATION INCORPORATED	Cereal Box Weaving Loom	1	1. 1
	Creative Castaways	1 2 / 1 2 3	
	Graphic Notation and Musical Instruments	1 / 1 2 / 1 2 3	1. 1 2 2. 1 2 3. 1 2 4. 1 2 3
	Balloon Bass Guitar	1	
	Box Harp	1	
	Buzzy Harmonica	1	
	Drums	1	1. 1 2. 1
	Kazoo	1	
	Rockin' Cereal Box Guitar	1	
	Shakers	1	1. 1
	Straw Pan Flute	1	
	Tweeter	1	
	Look and Find	1 2 / 1 2 3	

CHAPTER	ACTIVITY	GAME PLAY	VARIATIONS
4: AMALGAMATION INCORPORATED continued	Puppet		
	Story Cards		1.
	Tangrams		

CHAPTER	ACTIVITY	GAME PLAY	VARIATIONS
5: LINKS AND CHAINS	CapWords		1.
	Fishing Match		1.
	Get the Picture?		1. 2.
	It's in the Bag		1. 2. 3. 4.
	Jianzi		2. 3.
	Order Up!		
	Play Money		1. 2.
	Rock-n-Roll Math		
	Shape Toss		

CHAPTER	ACTIVITY	GAME PLAY	VARIATIONS
5: LINKS AND CHAINS **continued**	Similarities		
	Up and Down the Number Line		

CHAPTER	ACTIVITY	GAME PLAY	VARIATIONS
6: SPINNING, ROLLING, FLOATING	Buoyancy or Bust		
	Kite		
	Mini Spinnies		1.
	Pint-Sized Parachute		
	Pinwheel		
	Rain Stick		1.
	Toothpaste Box Glider		1.
	Tubes of Fun		1.
	Twirlybird		
	T'wis		1.
	'Ulu Maika		
	Whizzer		

Glossary of Materials and Terms

Aluminum foil: Rather than throw away that used piece of foil, wash it with soap and water, and reuse it for green play

Angler: A person who fishes using a rod and reel

Balloons: Regular-sized, latex balloons in any color; balloons of different shapes or materials will be specified in the supply list

Bamboo skewer: Round bamboo stick used for kabobs

Bow: The front of a boat, canoe, or ship

Cardinality: A math term in reference to the number of items in a given set

Cereal box: Reuse any size cereal box for the activities in this book; larger boxes will just create larger projects

Craft sticks: Wooden sticks that resemble those found in frozen treats (Note: Used frozen treat sticks are very difficult to sanitize, thus are NOT recommended.)

Darts: A game where players have three chances to throw a dart at a board with concentric circles, with sections of the board indicating different point values. The objective of the game is different depending on the game; players can either start with a certain number of points [501 points is typical (Masters Games)] and points are subtracted from this total, or players start at zero and add up their points until they reach a point level.

Drinking straw: When no other dimensions are specified, assume this means that any straw is acceptable, including ones that bend

Egg cartons: Only use foam egg cartons that have been sterilized with a bleach/water solution. Cartons not sanitized run the risk of having the salmonella bacteria. Cartons made from paper-based product must NOT be used as they cannot be sanitized.

Exchange: The trading of money, goods, or services with people in order to receive goods or services

Exchange rate: How much one set of currency is worth in another country's set of currency

File folders (used): Manila folders with tabs; can substitute unmarked pocket folders

Large eraser: Parallelogram eraser that removes pencil markings

Mailer cards: The 4-in x 6-in (10.2-cm x 15.2-cm) cards that come in magazines (such as subscription cards)

Ordinality: A number indicating its place in a series or sequence, such as first, second, or third

Paper clips: Unless otherwise specified, use standard #1-size metal clips

Paper lunch bag: Standard size is best: 10 in x 5 in x 3 in (25.4 cm x 12.7 cm x 7.6 cm)

Paper/strips of paper/scraps of paper: Scrap printer or notebook paper work particularly well in these projects

Paper tube: Paper towel or wrapping paper tube

Plastic bottle cap: A 12- to 16-oz (354.9- to 473.2-mL) plastic water or soda bottle cap

Plastic cap: Larger, softer cap from a plastic gallon of milk or juice

Plastic cup: When size is not specified, any plastic cup will work, such as a yogurt, gelatin, pudding, or other single-serving container

Plastic deli container: Round container obtained at the counter (usually come in half-pint, pint, and quart sizes); NOT containers from pre-packaged meats

Plastic water bottle: Disposable, one-serving bottle

Play day: A day that is set aside for play or an event comprised of playful activities. The purpose of a play day is to draw attention to the importance and benefits of play and recreation. The United Kingdom celebrates a national "Playday" the first Wednesday of August (National Children's Bureau, 2007).

Quadrants: Four equal sections

Rain stick: A tubular rattle

Rubber bands: When size is not specified, a standard-sized rubber band will do (not the thick ones that come around some vegetables and not the tiny ones used for braces or jewelry)

Ruler: A tool for measuring length (all measurements in this book are in U.S. standard units with metric conversions following in parentheses)

Shuttle: A device used in weaving to hold the weft and move it over and under the strings of the warp. As the shuttle moves across the warp, the weft is gradually released from the shuttle.

Shuttlecock: A cone-shaped object that is batted back and forth over a net in the game badminton. A shuttlecock is often referred to as a "birdie."

Tagboard: Thin, cardboard packaging material like that of a cereal box

Tangrams: An old, shape-dissecting puzzle whose exact origin is unknown. The puzzle has enjoyed resurgences of popularity as the centuries pass, as it appeals to people on a number of levels (mathematically, artistically, historically, etc.).

Tape: Specific kind does not matter unless specified

Timbre: The sound or quality of a voice or instrument that distinguishes it from another voice or instrument

Tin can lids: ONLY use lids that have been removed with a safety opener and thus have smooth edges. NEVER use lids with sharp or jagged edges.

Tissue box: Traditional style with a hole in the center of a panel; avoid those that have openings on the corners of the box

Trinkets: Small, colorful items or toys added to the Look-and-Find game (see page 104); for example, animal figurines, play food, play utensils (forks, spatulas, spoons), or balls

Warp: A term used in weaving to refer to the strings held in place on a loom

Weft: A term used in weaving to refer to the thread that is woven over and under the strings of the warp

Wicket: A wooden stick that serves as the target in the game cricket

Bibliography

AbleMedia (2000). *Ancient Africa*. Retrieved March 4, 2014 from http://ablemedia.com/ctcweb/consortium/vamafrica.html

Benefits of Play. (n.d.). *Play = Learning*. Retrieved April 8, 2011 from http://udel.edu/~roberta/play/benefits.html

Brandt, R. (1993). *On teaching for understanding: A conversation with Howard Gardner*. Retrieved January 20, 2014 from: http://www.ascd.org/publications/educational-leadership/apr93/vol50/num07/On-Teaching-for-Understanding@-A-Conversation-with-Howard-Gardner.aspx

Brown, S. (2010). *Play: how it shapes the brain, opens the mind, and invigorates the soul*. NY: Avery.

BTHA Play Leaflets—British Toy and Hobby Association and Toy Fair RSS (2010). Making Time for Toys. Retrieved February 1, 2011 from http://www.maketime2play.co.uk/

Calia, S. (1891). Street games of boys in Brooklyn, New York. *The Journal of American Folklore* 4(3), 221-227.

Culin, S. (1960). *Games of the Orient*. Rutland, VT: Charles E. Tuttle Company.

Dewey, J. (1907). *The school and society*. Chicago: The University of Chicago Press, 47–73.

Elliott Avedon Virtual Museum of Games (2010). *Hawaiian Games*. Retrieved August 17, 2012 from http://gamesmuseum.uwaterloo.ca/Archives/Culin/Hawaii1899

Elliott Avedon Virtual Museum of Games (2010). *Inuit Bone Gambling Game and Puzzle*. Retrieved August 17, 2012 from http://gamesmuseum.uwaterloo.ca/VirtualExhibits/Inuit/english/bagbone.html

Enchanted Learning (2003). *The US One Dollar Bill*. Retrieved January 14, 2014 from http://www.enchantedlearning.com/math/money/bills/one/

Erikson, E.H. (1950). *Childhood and society*. New York: Norton.

Frost, J. L., Wortham, S.C., & Reifel, S.C. (2008). *Play and child development*. 3 ed. Upper Saddle River: Pearson.

Ginsburg, K.R. (2007). The importance of play in promoting healthy child development and maintaining strong parent-child bonds. *Pediatrics* 119(1), 182–191.

Good, A. (2012). *Knucklebones*. Retrieved August 17, 2012 from http://archaeologicalmuseum.jhu.edu/the-collection/object-stories/archaeology-of-daily-life/childhood/knucklebones/

Gopnik, A. (2012). Let the children play, it's good for them! *Smithsonian Magazine*. Retrieved January 20, 2014 from http://www.smithsonianmag.com/science-nature/Let-the-Children-Play-Its-Good-for-Them.html

Grunfeld, F. V. (1975). *Games of the world: how to make them, how to play them, how they came to be*. New York: Holt, Rinehart and Winston.

Hughes, F. P. (2010). *Children, play, and development*. 4th ed. Los Angeles: Sage.

Johnson, J. E., Christie, J.F. & Wardle, F. (2005). *Play, Development, and Early Education*. Boston: Pearson, 2005.

Jung, C. G. (1923). *Psychological types; or, The psychology of individuation*. London: Paul, Trench, Trubner.

Masters Games. (2012). *Rules of Darts*. Retrieved March 14, 2014 from http://www.mastersgames.com/rules/darts-rules.htm

National Children's Bureau (2007). *About Playday* Retrieved January 20, 2014 from http://www.playday.org.uk/about-playday.aspx

Pan, S. J., & Yang, Q. (2010). A Survey on Transfer Learning. *IEEE Transactions on Knowledge and Data Engineering*, 22(10), 1345-1359.

Piaget, J. (1962). *Play, dreams and imitation* (Vol. 24). New York: Norton.

Prindle, T. (2013). Bundle & Pin Game. *Native American Technology and Art*. Retrieved July 31, 2013 from http://www.nativetech.org/games/bundle&pin.html

Schleyer, C. (2013). *How to Play Kickball*. Retrieved December 14, 2013 from http://www.kids-sports-activities.com/how-to-play-kickball.html

Sharpe, A. S. (1991). *John Dewey: the collected works*, 1882-1953; index. Carbondale: Southern Illinois University Press.

Sierra, J. & Kaminski, R. (1995). *Children's traditional games: games from 137 countries and cultures*. Phoenix: Oryx Press, 75.

Timin, A. (2008). Picturing Music: The Return of Graphic Notation. *NewMusicBox*. Retrieved June 16, 2011 from http://www.newmusicbox.org/articles/Picturing-Music-The-Return-of-Graphic-Notation/

Toth, Jay (2008). *The Winter Game of Snow Snake*. Retrieved February 1, 2011 from http://www.uwlax.edu/mvac/knowledge/NAGames.htm

United States Mint (2014). *Coin Specifications*. Retrieved January 15, 2014 from http://www.usmint.gov/about_the_mint/?action=coin_specifications

Vygotsky, L. (1966). Play and its role in the mental development of the child. Voprosy psikhologii, No. 6, pp. 1–18.

Maupin House *by*
capstone
professional

At Maupin House by Capstone Professional, we continue to look for professional development resources that support grades K–8 classroom teachers in areas, such as these:

Literacy	Language Arts
Content-Area Literacy	Research-Based Practices
Assessment	Inquiry
Technology	Differentiation
Standards-Based Instruction	School Safety
Classroom Management	School Community

If you have an idea for a professional development resource, visit our Become an Author Web Site at:

http://maupinhouse.com/index.php/become-an-author

There are two ways to submit questions and proposals.
1. You may send them electronically to:
   http://maupinhouse.com/index.php/become-an-author
2. You may send them via postal mail. Please be sure to include a self-addressed stamped envelope for us to return materials.